THE BIOGRAPHY OF
PRESIDENT VON HINDENBURG

THE MACMILLAN COMPANY
NEW YORK · BOSTON · CHICAGO · DALLAS
ATLANTA · SAN FRANCISCO

MACMILLAN & CO., Limited
LONDON · BOMBAY · CALCUTTA
MELBOURNE

THE MACMILLAN COMPANY
OF CANADA, Limited
TORONTO

PRESIDENT VON HINDENBURG

THE BIOGRAPHY OF
PRESIDENT VON HINDENBURG

BY

RUDOLPH WETERSTETTEN
AND
A. M. K. WATSON

NEW YORK
THE MACMILLAN COMPANY
1930

SET UP BY BROWN BROTHERS LINOTYPERS
PRINTED IN THE UNITED STATES OF AMERICA
BY THE FERRIS PRINTING COMPANY

ILLUSTRATIONS

THE BIOGRAPHY OF
PRESIDENT VON HINDENBURG

THE BIOGRAPHY OF
PRESIDENT VON HINDENBURG

CHAPTER I

Towards the end of the eighteenth century, King Frederick William of Prussia was graciously pleased to sanction the union of the names and arms of the two old military families von Beneckendorff and von Hindenburg. The Beneckendorffs had been famous soldiers for over seven centuries; the von Hindenburgs are first mentioned in history in the year 1208. The union of the two families in the eighteenth century was based on the marriage of Hans Joachim von Beneckendorff, a man of poor health, with Scholastica von Hindenburg, the daughter of a house, ancient and noble indeed, but threatened with extinction. Scholastica's only brother, Otto Friedrich von Hindenburg, a soldier, lived for twenty-five years without being called upon to face the real business of his profession. At the end of this time, he fought in the two Silesian wars, and had his leg shattered by a cannon ball, so that he was obliged to retire in 1579. The King, at whose side he had fought, rewarded him with the gift of two estates, Limbsee and Neudeck. It seems possible that Otto Friedrich von Hindenburg may have called to his house his sister's son, Christoph Wilhelm von Beneckendorff. The latter left the Prussian army with the rank of

[1]

captain, married Katherina Tugendreich von Brandt, heiress to two estates, and devoted himself to the management of the property. He and his brother, Johann Daniel, sold their shares in the estates of which they became possessed when their parents died. Johann Daniel remained without issue. The von Beneckendorff family, after the sale of these estates in Neumark, remained settled in Prussia.

In 1747, Johann Otto Gottfried von Beneckendorff was born. He also adopted a military career, which, like his father, he early abandoned to devote himself to estate management. However, on the death of Margarethe von Hindenburg (sole heiress of her brother Otto Friedrich), who left everything to her sister's grandson, he gave up his former possessions, settled on the two properties of Limbsee and Neudeck, and accepted the condition that he should unite the name and arms of von Hindenburg with his own. He married Louisa von Eulenburg, daughter of a famous Prussian family, and had two sons by her. The elder, after a distinguished military career, died, without male heirs, in 1847. The second son, Otto Ludwig, born in 1778, also became an officer, but he soon tired of military life, and, with his wife Eleonore von Brederlow, took up his residence at Neudeck, which he acquired from his father in 1801.

The property of Limbsee was sold in 1833, and Neudeck remained henceforth the true home of the von Hindenburgs. Otto Ludwig and his wife had fourteen children, who were brought up with the Spartan simplicity usual in the family of a Prussian officer; a simplicity which, in this case, was perhaps heightened to some extent by the terror of the Napoleonic Wars and the period of suffering which they brought to Germany. The youngest son of this numerous family, Robert, was born at Neudeck in 1816, and was destined to become a distinguished officer and the father of Paul von Beneckendorff and von Hindenburg, the second President of the German Republic.

With fourteen children to bring up, it was plain that the estate of Neudeck could hardly afford great luxury to its possessor. Albert, the fourth son, married the daughter and heiress of the owner of a neighboring property, and devoted himself to agriculture. For the sake of tradition, however, the army was the career which the sons were expected to adopt. The youngest boy, Robert, at the age of sixteen, entered the 18th Regiment of Foot, in the year 1832. He was a sensitive youth, a little inclined to melancholy, and he cherished a deep devotion for his home and for the amenities of home life. He soon learned to love his profession and was known to be unusually capable and conscientious in the carrying out of his duties. In 1845 he married Luise Schwickart, daughter of a military surgeon, a man who bore a high reputation in Prussia and who had been awarded the Iron Cross for very distinguished conduct on the battlefield.

To Robert and Luise, on October 2, 1847, their first son was born in the town of Posen. This boy, destined to become world-famous, and to be the just admiration of both friend and foe, was given the names Paul Ludwig Hans Anton. The shadow of war hung over him even in his infancy, for the Polish Rebellion of 1848 broke out in the year following his birth. The town of Posen, which, together with Danzig and certain other places, had, in the days of

Catherine II of Russia, been handed over to Prussia at the Second Partition of Poland, was left unguarded, the garrison having been sent into the field to suppress the rising. Mieroslawski [1] was able to enter the town. Hindenburg tells us, in his book of memoirs,[2] that his mother, forced, as were all inhabitants of Posen, to illuminate her house in honor of the Polish leader, sat in a back room at the cradle of her little son, and comforted herself with the reflection that, in her heart, the lights in her front windows were burning in honor of the King of Prussia's birthday, which happened to fall upon that day. Mieroslawski's triumph was but a transient one, for the Prussians put down the rebellion with great rigor, and it was followed by trials and condemnations to death and imprisonment.

Robert and Luise von Hindenburg had three more children: a son, Otto, just under two years younger than Paul, who died in 1908; a sister four years younger; and a still younger brother, Bernhard, who has written a biography of von Hindenburg.

In the year 1850, Robert was appointed company commander in the militia, and the little family removed from Posen to Pinne. Here they settled in a small house with a big garden, and the children passed their early years in a healthy country environment. In 1855, Robert was transferred to Glogau as captain and company commander, and here Frau Schwickart, Paul's maternal grandmother, came to join her daughter and her family.

It was in Glogau that Paul went to school; at first to the little evangelical *Burgerschule*, and later to the Royal *Gym-*

---

[1] Leader of the Polish Rebellion in Prussia.
[2] *Aus meinem Leben.*

nasium,[1] which, however, he left in his second year to go to the military academy. On the first page of his *Aus meinem Leben*, Paul von Hindenburg says that "to become a soldier was not a decision for me—it was a matter of course." So, a little eleven-year-old boy "not without fears" passed through the iron gates of the military school in Wahlstatt (in Silesia) and shamefacedly dashed away the unbidden tears that the parting with his father had brought into his eyes, knowing that it would never do to disgrace the new cadet's jacket. There was nothing soft about the life of the Prussian cadet corps in the time of von Hindenburg's youth. Discipline was severe, the life, as he himself says, "consciously and purposely rough."

The boy seems to have been quite an ordinary sort of boy, with nothing in particular to distinguish him from his fellows or to point to the high destiny he was to fulfil. He appears to have conceived the highest admiration for certain of the masters in the cadet school and to have thrown himself eagerly into the general life of the place. It is certain that the hard, healthy existence of this period counteracted the effects of a serious illness which Paul had suffered as a small boy and the further weakening effects of too rapid growth. In consequence of these physical drawbacks, he was a little late in developing and showed no special inclination to apply himself diligently to study. Little by little, however, his ambition awoke, and he finished his education bearing the reputation of an unusually gifted scholar.

As was generally the case with the royal cadets, a close and firm loyalty and love for the King and the royal house-

---

[1] Approximating to the English "public school" and to the American "preparatory school," save that there are no boarders.

hold was rooted in von Hindenburg's heart; and, to him, a cadet's parade which took place in 1859 before Prince Friedrich Wilhelm (later the Emperor) and his wife was a great and exciting experience.

In 1863, having reached *Sekunda*,[1] von Hindenburg was transferred to Berlin, to the cadet school in Neue Friedrichstrasse. In 1864, the war against Denmark broke out, and a letter written by him on May the 31st of that year serves to show very clearly what type of boy he had developed into. His stern upbringing in Wahlstatt had not hardened his nature; it had merely increased his lively affection for his parents and his home.

Recently I got your welcome letter, or rather that of dear Papa, which to a certain extent quieted me. That you, dear Mama, should be so ill pains me deeply, but I hope you are better already and that we may look forward to a rapid convalescence. Only take good care of yourself and don't overstrain yourself too early, in your care for others. Forgive me for permitting myself to make regulations for you, but you surely know how worried I am about you. I already had a premonition that you were very ill; I dreamed about it all night, and thought about it in the daytime, without ever having had any news. God will certainly hear our prayer and keep and strengthen you. Last Wednesday was the Spring Parade down Unter den Linden; as usual we came first and then looked on. Next day, his Majesty sent to tell us he was satisfied with our march past and to say how he and all the princes reckoned it as a high credit to us that the cadets entering the army had hurried off at once to Schleswig [2] without waiting for their equipment. Three cadets took part in the charge still dressed in our uniform; one of them recently sent his things back. A non-commissioned officer [3] is wearing the jacket now, so that we have it always before our eyes. Prince Carl told how, after the charge, he had asked a bombardier whether he felt tired, to which he answered, "How can I be tired when our officers

[1] The highest class but one in a German school.
[2] To take part in the war with Denmark.
[3] Selected cadets held non-commissioned rank over their comrades.

are so gallant and our young cadets lead the way for us so bravely?" The King has ordered that all this be written in our archives.

Hindenburg made many friends as a cadet, giving to these, and demanding from them, that absolute loyalty and sincerity which were characteristic of him.

In 1865, he had the honor of being appointed a page to the widowed Queen Elizabeth and thus had the opportunity of seeing something of the pomp of life at the Court. This service strengthened, if that were possible, his love for the Prussian royal house, and the gold watch which his mistress gave him accompanied him through three wars.

The war with Denmark in 1864 wrought up the royal cadets to a high pitch of excitement, and von Hindenburg and his other comrades who were still too young to go into the field saw their more fortunate companions off with a wistful envy and accompanied their departure with the warmest of good wishes. Many of these were to live to see the darkest hour in the history of their country—but to von Hindenburg it was to be given to stand as the great representative of a completely changed Germany, a Germany bankrupt of all the royal pomp and military power with which his education had been identified.

Before leaving the cadet corps, von Hindenburg and other students of his year were taken to the palace and formally introduced to the King. Each boy had to tell his name and the rank of his father—some of the more nervous making a sorry business of this ceremony. The King spoke a few serious words to these young, eager boys, and told them that they must always do their duty, no matter how hard it might seem.

In this spring of 1865, Paul von Hindenburg passed his

final examination, acquitting himself with distinction; and in the spring of the following year, he left the cadet school and on April 7, 1866, at the age of eighteen and a half, he joined the 3rd Infantry Regiment of Guards.

With what deep affection and gratitude Paul von Hindenburg looked back upon his cadet days is revealed in a letter which he sent in the first year of the war to the commandant of the cadet school at Wahlstatt. He wrote then:

> If I have achieved much in my military career, I have always been conscious that the basis of my success is to be sought in my education in the cadet corps. If enthusiasm for my future calling and love for King and country had already been implanted in my child's heart in the home of my parents, so, in the cadet corps, comradeship, self-control and discipline were inculcated into the growing boy and youth.
>
> It is no wonder that, as a grey-haired man, I still think with a grateful heart of the years spent in the cadet corps, although the times then were certainly rougher than they are now. But those times formed character and created men who never lacked initiative or responsibility.
>
> I know that today's milder ways of education—even though it be, now and then, by other paths—lead to the same result. Our brave young officers show that daily on the battlefields. And so I wish, for each one of your cadets, that he may look back upon his cadet years with as thankful a heart as I do, that he may be able to keep his heart young and fresh through all the storms of life, and that he may go as far as possible in his military career.

Hindenburg's father retired in 1863, with the rank of major, and settled down to a quiet life at Neudeck, though he was destined to serve again, and before very long, in the Prussian army.

CHAPTER II

THE 3rd Infantry Regiment of Guards, which von
Hindenburg now joined, as he tells us in his *Aus meinem
Leben*, had been re-established by reason of the increase of
active military units in the years 1859-60. The new regiment
had won honor in the war of 1864; and the Prussian soldier
looked upon the honor of his regiment as upon his own
personal honor: the two were one thing, to be jealously protected to the death. Hindenburg bears testimony to the
fact that this pride of the soldiers in their regiment was so
strong that nothing could break it, not even the constant
depletion of the ranks (as in such a war as the last) and the
re-building of them with fresh blood. The torch of honor
passed from the hands of the dying men to their successors
and was, in turn, held high by them until death forced them
to relinquish it.

In the year in which Hindenburg entered his regiment
as a lieutenant, the war with Austria broke out, and on June
28, 1866, he went into action for the first time at Soor. His
feelings on this occasion are described in a letter to his
parents in which he said:

First, a certain pleasure that one is at last going to smell powder,
but then a worried anxiety as to whether, as a young officer, one will
be able to do one's duty satisfactorily. Then, when one hears the
first shots (which are always greeted with a cheer), one is gripped
with a kind of enthusiasm; a short prayer, a thought for the loved
ones at home, and forward!

[9]

Hindenburg himself was not much engaged in this first battle, and was concerned only in a little sharpshooting in a wood and the taking of a few prisoners. His company belonged to the reserve, which never reached the front of the battle. On the following day, however, he was made acquainted with the other side of the picture, and was sent out with sixty grenadiers to look for and bury the dead. This duty was made all the more difficult because the grain had not been cut, and he had some difficulty in getting back to his company in the afternoon, by which time the whole division had started on its southward march.

The Prussian army, which had marched into Bohemia in three divisions, united victoriously in the decisive battle of Königgrätz, and it was here that von Hindenburg had his first real taste of battle and gained his first honor, the *Rote Adlerorden* (Order of the Red Eagle) Fourth Class. As a young man he once said: "My keenest wish would be to stand at the head of a regiment, and to lead it hurrahing against the foe;" and he added, after a pause, "It would mean everything to me!" Here, at Königgrätz, he was to show that he was indeed a born soldier and a born leader of men. The archives of the regiment tell the story of the fight at the village of Rosberitz, in terse, soldier's language:

Grape-shot was suddenly fired at Lieutenant von Hindenburg's rifle-men. A battery had been hurriedly brought along from Rosberitz and had opened fire on this division at close quarters. After a short volley, Lieutenant von Hindenburg threw himself upon the gun. A grape-shot grazed his head and, for a moment, he fell stunned. When he sprang to his feet again, he saw that three guns were already in the hands of his men, while two others were being got away in the direction of Wsestar. These two, which were caught in a narrow defile between Rosberitz and Sweti, were also captured by the fifth company.

That this young man was an ardent enthusiast and that he had not learned to know the miseries and horrors that war brings in its train can be seen from a letter written to his parents at about this time.

For a soldier war is a normal circumstance, and in addition I am in God's hands. If I fall, that is the most honorable and most beautiful death; a wound, also, can only be for the best; and if I return unscathed—well, all the better.

Of his wound, he wrote to his parents:

A bullet passed through the eagle of my helmet, grazed my head without wounding me severely, and went out again behind the eagle. I fell down unconscious and my men surrounded me, thinking I was dead. Had it been half an inch deeper, the bullet would have entered my brain and I should have lain there cold and dead.

Hindenburg's father was also active in this war, as Knight of Honor of the Order of St. John. In caring for wounded men in the hospitals, he came face to face with the darker side of fighting. Also, he was an older man, and it is small wonder that his letters to his wife bore striking contrast to those written by his son. Addressing Frau von Hindenburg, he wrote:

O God, what a rod of punishment in Thy hand is this torch of war! Praised be Jesus Christ that He so graciously protects our beloved child and has not brought him to these rooms where pictures of misery meet one and where tears of agony have been shed so often and must long continue to flow.

Königgrätz was a decisive victory, but it was a fierce and savage fight. At one point the division with which von Hindenburg fought was obliged to retreat, as it was able to do only under the cover provided by a burning thatched roof, which fell from the house into the street and prevented pursuit. The companies were soon brought into order again and supports approached from the rear. The Prussians then rapidly occupied the village, which the enemy troops evacuated to join in the general rout of their whole army.

Much has been written to show that the Prussian officer has not much understanding of his men and that there is little bond of comradeship between them. In this connection there is an interesting story about von Hindenburg, Many years later, when Hindenburg was appointed field marshal, he received a letter from a veteran of Königgrätz, wishing him luck. A day or two later, the old soldier received a postcard from the field marshal, written in his own hand, with these words:

Many thanks for your letter, which unfortunately I can answer only briefly because of the many claims on my time. I am glad that you remember your leader at Königgrätz and I still think often and with pleasure about those times. May it go well with you in your life's evening! That is the wish of your regimental comrade.

A money order came with the same post, bearing the message:

Please spend this sum in drinking a toast to the health of our most gracious Kaiser and King and to our dear old regiment. With a comrade's greetings.

VON HINDENBURG.

When peace was made, the 3rd Regiment of Guards was garrisoned at Hanover, where von Hindenburg's company commander was a severe disciplinarian, a certain Captain von Seel, under whom he learned to drill recruits.

The town of Hanover became so dear to Hindenburg that he settled there after his retirement. Many of the inhabitants were at first hostile towards the Prussians, but von Hindenburg says that the loyalty of the Hanoverians towards their reigning house was never condemned by any of his comrades, although they were all impressed by the necessity of uniting Hanover with Prussia. The officers were soon received with pleasure by many of the townspeople, and von Hindenburg was very quick to respond to the *Gemüthlichkeit* which he felt around him. The beauty of the town and its environment made a strong appeal to him, and he was never dull in his spare hours, many of which he spent riding or walking in the surrounding woods.

In the summer of 1867, the King of Prussia visited Hanover for the first time, and von Hindenburg stood with the Guard of Honor before the palace. The King stopped and asked the young man how he had won his decoration,[1] a circumstance which naturally caused him much pride and pleasure.

The happy days of peace drew to an end, and war, "the normal condition for a soldier," once again broke out. Hindenburg, as adjutant of the 1st Battalion, went into the field in 1870 under the command of Major von Seegenberg, who had fought also in the wars of 1864 and 1866.

Hindenburg's regiment marched for many days in the blazing heat and covered with dust, until it reached the battlefield of Vionville on August 17. Here the men saw traces of the severity of the fight in which their 3d and 10th Army Corps had been engaged. The march was resumed

[1] The Order of the Red Eagle.

the next day, and the Prussian regiment was joined by the 12th (Saxon) Corps; towards midday the troops reached Doncourt. On this short march, from Vionville to Doncourt, the men suffered acutely owing to an insufficient water supply. Hindenburg visited the grave of his cousin, who had fallen at Vionville, in the cemetery of Mars la Tour, and rode over parts of the battlefield. In his *Aus meinem Leben,* he tells us that "rows, and, in places, even heaps of dead, French and Prussians intermingled . . . proved what a murderous conflict had been waged here and in the immediate neighborhood."

The regiment, having reached Doncourt, was tired out, and there was little enthusiasm among the men, who were sorely in need of rest. It seemed to them that they had come upon the scene too late, and the grueling march had been in vain. Suddenly, from the east, the thunder of guns was heard, a thunder which increased rapidly in volume. The 11th Army Corps had met the enemy. The march in a northeasterly direction was resumed, and their weariness immediately fell away from the soldiers. They were, after all, to face the French. Near Batilly, the order was given to unfurl the flags—an order which was greeted and obeyed with cheers. Batteries went galloping past the marching men, in the direction of the foe. "From minute to minute," says Hindenburg, "the feeling rose higher that a really great battle was to be fought." They could see great clouds of smoke, which hung on the hot, heavy air, arising from the gun emplacements. It was possible, at last, to make out more or less the positions of the French infantry and artillery, whose fire was murderously directed against the German

11th Army Corps, and it seemed as if their left wing were in danger of being overwhelmed by the French.

Hindenburg's regiment, avoiding, for the present, a frontal attack, advanced by a small, grass-grown declivity, northwards upon Ste. Marie sur Chênes. The village was attacked and occupied, and Hindenburg's division marched southwards towards St. Privat. A short rest followed—a strange sort of rest, with stray bullets from St. Privat bringing death and wounds to the German soldiers, who were in mass formation.

Hindenburg rode to Roncourt to reconnoitre, and found that village free from soldiers, but he saw French infantry in the quarries which lay to the east. The Saxons had not arrived. He returned to his men and led two companies to Roncourt, just in time to meet and repulse an attack from the quarries by the French. Covered by the action of these two companies, the others were able to advance upon St. Privat, and Hindenburg and his men followed when, later, the village of Roncourt was occupied by a part of the 12th Army Corps. At St. Privat the fight was terrible. The field of battle was broad and without cover, and the French by a devastating infantry fire sought to annihilate the advancing German troops. The French remained in St. Privat, which was easy to defend owing to its protective, sloping approach. At last came a lull in the fighting, for both sides were exhausted. Reinforcements (the 2nd Brigade of Guards) came up from Ste. Marie, and the Saxons drew in from the northwest. The sorely tried infantry, which had stood the brunt of the battle, drew fresh courage from the timely arrival of these supports. They stood up once more in the glow of the sunset and made a heroic, irresistible attack upon the village. As darkness fell, the French ranks broke in defeat—St. Privat was won, but at heavy cost. The 3rd Regiment of Guards had lost 36 officers and 1060 non-commissioned ranks and men, of whom 17 officers and 304 other ranks had been killed. Other Guards infantry regiments had suffered as severely. There was little time to reflect upon these losses; the dead were buried on the 19th of August, and the regiment marched westwards on the 20th. On the way, the divisional leader, Lt.-General von Pape, spoke to the men, and praised them for their gallant conduct on the field, saying:

Further, the old soldiers' saying holds good for us: "If there be thousands to the left, or thousands to the right, if all our friends fall, we will fight on." [1]

The Guards regiments drew up finally on the hills east of Gironne and watched from thence the battle of Sedan, in which, owing to their terrible losses, they were not permitted to take part. From the hills they saw how the French were surrounded, how they made valiant and repeated efforts to break through the circle that was rapidly closing in on them and how utter a defeat they had to suffer. Hindenburg joined in the singing of *Nun danket alle Gott,* and took part in the general rejoicings, for everyone thought that the war was over. In this, however, they were mistaken.

On September 2, the Crown Prince of Prussia visited the troops, and the King came to them later in the day. He was received with unparalleled delight and the men were not to be kept in ranks. Hindenburg says they surrounded the

[1] *Aus meinem Leben.*

monarch and kissed his hands and feet, while he thanked them with tears in his eyes for what they had done at St. Privat. Bismarck rode in the train of the King, and received a special cheer.

On September 3, Hindenburg's regiment was ordered to round up all Frenchmen who were outside Sedan, and drive them into the fortress. There were, however, so few of these that it was unnecessary for the regiment to do anything; a few patrols sufficed for the work. As Hindenburg turned back to make this announcement to a following regiment, he saw a cloud of dust on the road leading north. A French doctor told him that this cloud hid the Emperor Napoleon III with his guard of Black Hussars on his way to captivity.[1]

On the same evening, the regiments started the march to Paris, and on September 19, from the high ground about six miles northeast of St. Denis, they sighted the French capital. It was a clear autumn day, and the city looked eminently beautiful under the sunlight. Hindenburg wrote in his memoirs:[2]

I believe that the Crusaders must have looked upon Jerusalem with like feelings to those with which we beheld Paris lying at our feet.

And Paris, like Jerusalem, was to fall.

The regiment was quartered at Gonesse, where, more than half a century earlier, Blücher and Wellington had met to discuss tactics.

For months the German forces were encamped outside Paris, the monotony of existence being broken only

[1] Napoleon, taken prisoner at Sedan, was sent by the King of Prussia to the Castle of Wilhelmshöhe, near Kassel.
[2] *Aus meinem Leben.*

occasionally by sallies from the city on the part of the French.

For the next few months the states of the North German Union were engaged in negotiations with the southern states. Everyone had hoped, in consequence of the victory over the French, that these would gladly unite with the Northern Union to form one great country. But there were many difficulties to overcome. Discussions between the appropriate statesmen were opened at Munich in September but were broken off. They were resumed in October at Versailles. At last, on November 15, agreements were signed with Baden and Hesse. Bavaria and Württemberg made much trouble, but they, too, on the 23rd and 25th of November respectively, gave their signatures. Germany was united, at last, and the monarch was now German Kaiser and King of Prussia; and the new German Empire came into being.

So the month of January, 1871, brought Hindenburg one of the great experiences of his life, for he was ordered to Versailles to represent his regiment at the proclamation of the King of Prussia as German Emperor. He was deeply impresesd by the occasion and in his memoirs he pays tribute to the grace lent to it by the dignified bearing of the King. He also remarks that the south Germans threw themselves into the ceremony with more vigorous rejoicings than the Prussians, who, although feeling the greatness of the occasion just as strongly, acted with greater reserve. Even to this day, the difference in temperament between north and south Germans is very marked. The Prussians resemble the English, but the southerners, and more especially the Rhineland people, are enthusiastic, easily moved to laughter and tears.

Thus was the German Empire proclaimed in a foreign country and in time of war, and it was to fall a bare half-century later at the end of another and far more terrible war. In the evening, the new Kaiser gave a banquet to the generals who had attended the ceremony; and the junior officers dined as his guests in the Hôtel de France. And there was nothing, even then, to set Hindenburg out as a man apart from the other distinguished young men among whom he sat; no shadow of foreboding disturbed the warm loyalty he felt towards the King. He could not know that the little Prince Wilhelm, who eagerly followed the course of the war at home in Germany, would be the last of the German Kaisers and would live to see his erstwhile field marshal recognized as the paramount figure of the country. But many years were to pass before this change took place.

On January 19, the day after the proclamation, the sound of artillery called the guests from the picture gallery of Versailles back to their posts. The French were making their last brave effort—the sally of Mont Valérien, under Trochu; the capitulation of Paris followed on the 26th and the cessation of hostilities on the 28th. After the surrender of Paris, Hindenburg's brigade moved into pleasant quarters opposite the city on the banks of the Seine, in the neighborhood of Pont de Neuilly.

Hindenburg, Prussian to the depths of his being, was nevertheless undistinguished by the suspicion towards foreigners that unfortunately characterizes so many Englishmen. Young as he was, he was deeply impressed by the valiant spirit shown by the French, though later he was to deplore the conduct of some towards prisoners in the World War. He found something very magnificent in the endurance shown by a people, naturally emotional and ardent, in this war. He took the opportunity to ride through Paris and to observe not only the architecture and the monuments, but also the attitude of the French.

On March 3, the Corps of Guards paraded before the Kaiser at Longchamps. The spirit of patriotism for the Fatherland and veneration for the house of Hohenzollern ran high in the ranks of these Prussian soldiers. This was, perhaps, the "militarism" which later was to become so detested, both by the Germans themselves and by their enemies. It was at least founded upon a feeling which every Englishman should be able to understand—love for King and country. The tragedy was that this fresh, spontaneous feeling later became simply a ritual which was drilled not only into the army but into the civil population by means of a cast-iron discipline. The birthday of the Kaiser on March 22, celebrated by the army before Paris, supplied the occasion for another demonstration of loyalty and affection on the part of the troops.

Although the peace preliminaries had been ratified on March 2, and, on March 3, a part of the German army had begun its homeward journey, and although the Kaiser left Versailles on the 7th, von Hindenburg remained with the occupation army and was a witness of some of the disturbances which broke out in the French capital. The communists, who led the riots against the government, had no very hard task to· inflame a defeated people against its rulers. Fires, plunder and murder were the order of the day, and a sad procession of fugitives from the city kept the German troops informed about the situation. Hindenburg says [1] that on May 23 he received the impression that the whole of Paris was falling into destruction. He gives also a rather grimly amusing instance of the enterprise displayed by commercially minded men in turning any set of circumstances to their own advantage. Certain of these gentlemen erected telescopes on the hills to the northwest of Paris, and rented them to the German soldiers so that they might watch the progress of the civil war. Hindenburg, however (who scorned the telescopes), saw the end of the communists for the time being from a high window in St. Denis. The government's troops stormed Montmartre and swept away the last defences of the rebels.

At the beginning of June, Hindenburg returned with his regiment to Berlin, and, on the 16th of that month citizens of that beflagged and festively decorated capital were able to cheer the triumphal entry of the Kaiser and his victorious army. In the procession rode a young guards officer wearing the Iron Cross he had won at St. Privat.

[1] *Aus meinem Leben.*

CHAPTER III

AFTER the war, Hindenburg was able to spend some little time in rest and recuperation in his home at Neudeck. His parents, deeply grateful to have him safely back again, could not do enough to render his vacation enjoyable. His regiment was again stationed at Hanover, where he rejoined it after his visit to Neudeck. He remained here in service for the next few years, but then indulged his inclination to learn something of higher military affairs and set about getting ready to enter the *Kriegsakademie* (War Academy) to which he was admitted in 1873.

Hindenburg's first year at the *Kriegsakademie* caused him some disappointment. He had little patience with any study of which he could not see the immediate practical value. Even at the present day he regards a close study of classical antiquity as a waste of time for a man who has his living to make. For this reason he abhorred having to direct his attention, in those early days of his life, to ancient history and ancient military tactics, which, with the changed methods of warfare, could not be applied to war as he knew it. Moreover he was obliged to attend lectures in advanced mathematics; he wrote later [1] that only a few of the students who attended these classes found any practical use for their learning. The two following years of study, however,

[1] *Aus meinem Leben.*

brought Hindenburg much satisfaction. His teachers were men of mark and knew how to interest their classes. Tactics were his favorite study, and one of his professors, Lt.-Colonel Pochhammer, once wrote:

"Hindenburg always had some section of the General Staff's map before him, upon which he would begin to work quietly when the lecturer could not manage to interest him."

Years later, Hindenburg wrote to Pochhammer thanking him for what he owed him, and adding, "If I now and then turned away from the art of fortification to devote myself to tactics, you must kindly excuse it, because I have always adhered to the principle: *At the most important point, one cannot be too strong.* But I hope that the history of the war [1] will show that the art of fortification has often and faithfully served me in an emergency."

The three years spent at the *Kriegsakademie* slipped quickly away, and Hindenburg was ordered to the General Staff in the spring of 1877, and soon afterwards, in 1878, he was appointed second officer of the General Staff to the 2d Army Corps at Stettin. At this time Field Marshal Graf Moltke was the chief of the General Staff of the German army, and exercised an enormous personal influence not only upon those officers immediately atached to his own staff, but upon every officer in the whole of the General Staff. Those who held appointments on the General Staff were the very pick and flower of the army. It was not possible for a young officer to enter the *Kriegsakademie* unless he had acquitted himself with honor in his regiment and could produce a strong recommendation from his colonel. In his memoirs

[1] 1914-1918.

von Hindenburg speaks with the greatest admiration both of the General Staff and of the system from which it had been evolved.

"I believe," he writes, finally, "that the German General Staff as a whole understood the carrying out of its difficult task. Its performances until the end were masterly, even if a few faults and errors may have occurred. I could think of no more honorable testimony to its abilities than the fact that the foe demanded its dissolution, as one of the conditions for peace."

Hindenburg, with his interest in tactics and his great powers of administration, was eminently fitted to be a member of this important organization; although, at first, he was to be a little disappointed with the duties allotted to him. He tells us that, in addition to the higher work of the General Staff, its officers were also entrusted with the execution of a number of small matters of detail. As he was the youngest staff officer, his time was mostly occupied with such matters, which proved to be irksome only until he came to understand that this work was necessary for the welfare of the troops, and even necessary to the proper realization of the plans and ideas of his superiors. This work also supplied the foundation of that intimate knowledge of military technique and needs which was later to stand him in such good stead.

Hindenburg had always loved his home with an intensity which was probably increased by the fact that he had been obliged to leave it at so early an age; and it was not surprising, therefore, that his thoughts turned to marriage that he might recreate the atmosphere of his parents' house which he had grown to venerate. On September 24, 1879, Von Hindenburg married Gertrud Wilhelmine von Sperling, thirteen years his junior, and daughter of a distinguished soldier, Major-General von Sperling, who was appointed chief of the General Staff of the First Army after the outbreak of the war of 1870, but who died shortly after the cessation of hostilities. The marriage was ideally happy, and husband and wife were united in the closest mental and spiritual affinity. Their first child, a daughter, was born in 1880, and the small family was later increased by the addition of a son and another daughter.

In 1881, Hindenburg was transferred to Königsberg to the 1st Division, where he held an independent post on the General Staff. Here he was at first under the leadership of Lt.-General Nachtigall and later under General von Verdy du Vernois, who was afterwards Minister for War. Hindenburg was glad that he had been sent back to his own province; and the fact that he felt himself at home gave an additional impetus to his work. It was here, largely influenced by his brilliant superior, von Verdy, that Hindenburg extensively studied the questions relating to the defence of Germany on the east. Verdy, because he had been assigned to the headquarters of the Russian command during the Polish rising of 1863, was well informed regarding the political conditions on Germany's eastern frontier, and, in addition to this, he had an extraordinary knowledge of warfare. The period during which Hindenburg was in close connection with this man was one of inestimable value to him; he was to prove many years later, on the field of Tannenberg, how much he had profited by it. He remained at Königsberg for three years. His only son was born here in 1883.

In 1884, Hindenburg was again transferred, this time to frontier service with the 58th Infantry Regiment garrisoned at Fraustadt. Here he was in command of a company composed almost entirely of Poles. As the men, for the most part, knew little or no German and the officers could not speak Polish, the situation was peculiarly difficult. Hindenburg had picked up in childhood only a smattering of Polish, but he was not unsympathetic towards the men in his company. He found them industrious and willing to do their best; he also found gratitude and affection among them when they realized that their superiors were trying to smooth their path so far as possible. Hindenburg regarded the cases of petty thieving and drunkenness, which were regrettably frequent among the Poles, as attributable not so much to moral depravity as to improper upbringing and education. In this connection it must be remembered that Hindenburg, with his unusually broad outlook, was probably better served by the Poles than other officers were; for, owing to the language difficulty, the Poles suffered certain injustices in the army, which they bitterly resented.

Years later, when Hindenburg was commanding general of an army corps, an incident involving a Polish soldier occurred which is well worth recording. The general, when on duty, was always curt and severe and never permitted himself a joke or a smile. On this occasion he was inspecting the manœuvres of an infantry regiment. The captain of the 6th Company was worried, because the stupidest man in the regiment was among his charges. Being anxious to avoid trouble, he arranged with the sergeant-major to place the man—a Pole—at an outpost as far away as possible, in the hope that the general would find no reason to speak to him. The sergeant-major accompanied the man to the post and drilled him as to what he should answer if anyone should happen to speak to him. A wrong answer would cost him three days' confinement. The company commander, determined to avoid mishap, sent the sergeant-major cycling over to the post from time to time to see that the soldier had not forgotten his part. The inspection drew to a close when Hindenburg suddenly picked up a map and asked whether all approaches were properly guarded against the foe, demanding finally, "And hasn't this little track been forgotten?" "No," said the colonel. "Outpost No. 7 is there." Hindenburg glanced in the direction indicated, and then said, "Something seems to be out of order there. A soldier is riding about on a bicycle." Field-glasses were leveled, and the sergeant-major was seen cycling peacefully towards the outpost. Hindenburg entered his car and gave the order to drive to Outpost No. 7. The unhappy sentry was driven speechless with horror when he found himself the center of a number of officers. "Now, my son, what are you doing here all alone?" said Hindenburg, cheerfully, and, no answer being forthcoming, he added, "Well, well, if your general speaks to you, you must answer him. Or did you think, perhaps, that I should not come over here?" On hearing these words a broad grin spread over the Pole's face, and, in his queer dialect and using the familiar *Du,* he answered, "So that's what generals look like? The sergeant-major has already asked about you twice! He is sitting behind there in the cornfield!" There are occasions when even the sternest general must laugh—and this was one of them.

The time at Fraustadt passed very pleasantly. Hindenburg was delighted to be in close touch again with regimental duties and he found agreeable friends and acquaintances among the landed proprietors of the neighboring country. The intimate life of the little country town appealed to him greatly. He did his best to learn to know something about each one of his soldiers. For these reasons, in spite of the material advantages of returning to the General Staff, he left Fraustadt for Berlin in the summer of 1885 with deep regret. Here he became instructor in tactics at the *Kriegsakademie* and after a few months was promoted to major. On the General Staff, Major von Hindenburg was placed in the departments of Colonel Graf von Schlieffen and of Colonel Vogel von Falckenstein, the two most important departmental chiefs of their time. Here, for over a year, he was engaged in discussing plans for active operations. In the spring of 1886, practical field tests were made of the arrangements, in which Prince Wilhelm of Prussia [1] took part. It was the first meeting between the future warlord and his field marshal. In the winter following, the Prince was again present at a sham battle, on which occasion Hindenburg was in command of the "Russian" army.

Although, at the time when Hindenburg was in Berlin, Field Marshal von Moltke was leaving immediate contact with the different departments of the General Staff in the hands of his assistant, Hindenburg, who had an immeasurable admiration for Moltke, declares that his genius was still

[1] Afterwards Kaiser Wilhelm II.

everywhere to be felt. " . . . Graf Moltke enjoyed a unanimous, boundless veneration, and none of us could hold himself aloof from his influence." In private life Hindenburg sometimes came in contact with the great man, but they very rarely met officially. Although Moltke was an amiable and willing conversationalist and had a pleasant gift of humor, his public speeches were of the shortest.[1] In this connection Hindenburg has a good story to tell. On the Kaiser's birthday, the generals and staff officers were the guests of von Moltke. One of the officers offered to bet that Moltke's toast to the Kaiser would not be more than ten words, including the speech and the *Hoch*. The wager was accepted and the field marshal duly arose and said: *"Meine Herrn, der Kaiser hoch!"* The winner wished to renew the wager next year, but the loser had had enough. This time, however, he would have won, for on this occasion von Moltke used eleven words to propose the toast. In the year 1891 Hindenburg saw Moltke for the last time, as he lay dead. In paying tribute to one of the most remarkable figures in the history of Germany, Hindenberg writes:

The departed lay on his bier without the usual wig, so that the wonderful shape of his head was revealed. Only a wreath of laurels was required to complete the picture of an ideal Cæsar's head. How many mighty thoughts had been born in this brain; what high ideals had there held sway, and what noble and disinterested sentiments had been fostered there to the benefit of our Fatherland and its monarch. I am convinced our country has not since then produced one personality so great in soul and character—perhaps, indeed, Moltke was uniquely great in his development of these two attributes.

[1] Moltke was commonly called *Moltke der schweiger* (Moltke the silent) because of the brevity of his public speeches.

Three years before the death of Moltke, Hindenburg had sadly stood with the guard of honor that watched over the dead body of the first Kaiser under the high gray walls of the cathedral. Hindenburg still treasures a gray marble block cut out of the floor of the cathedral on the spot where the Emperor's coffin had rested. The old Emperor was very shortly followed to the grave by his son, the Kaiser Friedrich, who died before his time of a malignant tumor in the throat. At this time the General Staff was on a journey of inspection in the eastern part of Prussia, and it therefore happened that Hindenburg swore his oath of fidelity "on a spot where he was destined to prove it twenty-six years later."

Hindenburg carried out his duties as instructor in tactics in the *Kriegsakademie* for five years, along with much other heavy work. He was sometimes so busy that twenty-four hours seemed an insufficient span for each day's work. As an instructor he followed the methods he had earlier acquired from von Verdy. His pupils included many gifted young officers, among them two Turks (Shakir Bey and Tewfik Effendi) who later had distinguished military careers in their own country. At this time, Hindenburg was made chief General Staff officer of the 3rd Army Corps, where his chief was the younger General von Bronsart, who later became Minister for War, a post which had also been held by his elder brother.

In 1889, came another change, for General Verdy du Vernois became Minister for War and determined to bring his much valued junior into the ministry. Hindenburg was placed in charge of a section of the general War Department. Here he learned the "office work" side of soldiering, but it was unlikely that a man of his type—who so greatly preferred active regimental life to all other forms of existence —would devote himself with any pleasure to work carried on in an atmosphere of bureaucracy. Even, however, in the War Ministry he was able to find satisfaction in performing his task, and he conceived a great admiration for the way in which the various clerks and subordinates did their work. He himself had an enormous capacity for work, and the virtues of industry and efficiency always pleased him wherever he found them. The year 1893, however, extricated him from a situation which was really trying to him and returned him to his beloved soldiers. He was given the command of the 91st Infantry Regiment in Oldenburg. He was later to acknowledge the value to himself of the time spent in the ministry, but it was with unfeigned joy that he welcomed his new appointment and his return to a regiment. He writes [1] that "the post of commander of a regiment is the best in the army. The commander impresses his stamp upon the regiment, upon the bearers of the tradition of the army. His important tasks are the education of the officers not only from a service but from a social point of view and the training and guiding of the troops. I endeavored to implant a sense of chivalry in my officers and strict discipline in my battalions, and to encourage everywhere a quick assumption of duties, a pleasure in carrying them out, and a lively independence. The circumstance that the garrison consisted of infantry, cavalry and artillery gave me the opportunity to organize numberless manœuvres with mixed arms."

Hindenburg liked the town of Oldenburg and its in-

[1] *Aus meinem Leben.*

habitants who went so quickly and peacefully about their business, although a private sorrow, the death of his mother in August, 1893, clouded the first part of his residence there. He was very fond of his regiment, and he won the esteem and affection of the men. His great severity never set up barriers between him and his subordinates, for they knew that it proceeded only·from a desire to do the best he could for the honor of his regiment, a matter which lay as near to their hearts as it did to his.

February 18, 1896, the twenty-fifth anniversary of the founding of the German Empire at Versailles, was the occasion of many great festivities throughout the country. At Oldenburg, however, owing to the serious illness of the Grand Duchess Elizabeth, there could be no noisy rejoicings, though the army celebrated the occasion in a fitting manner, and Hindenburg delivered the speech of the day.

"The new German Empire," he said, "arose amid the thunder of guns. And soldiers' courage and soldiers' faith shall also protect and defend it, should any dare to lay hands upon this precious jewel, for which streams of soldiers' blood have been shed."

The following year Colonel von Hindenburg stepped into the barrack square for the last time, to say good-bye to the regiment. Addressing the men on this occasion, he said:

Musketeers! I am here to bid you farewell. I shall always look back with pleasure and pride upon the splendid time during which I have had the honor of standing at the head of the regiment, because, with a few exceptions, you have proved yourselves to be good, honorable soldiers. Take this spirit of faith and obedience with you into your homes, and it will go well with each of you. That is your old commander's wish to all of you. But, above all, I wish that the regiment shall preserve its old renown as well in peace as—if God should will—in the face of the foe. If I meet the regiment again in later time, I shall always rejoice. And now, as I linger among you for the last time, let us unite in the cheer which we gave together when I took over the command of the regiment more than three years ago.

The cheer for the Kaiser and the Grand Duke followed, and Hindenburg, after shaking hands with the sergeant-major, turned to the waiting men and called, "Adieu, musketeers!" Then he left the barrack square with their answering "adieu" ringing in his ears.

When he left Oldenburg in 1896, Hindenburg was to undergo a complete change of environment. He became chief of the General Staff of the 8th Army Corps at Coblenz. For the first time he was brought in touch with the people of the Rhineland. It must here be mentioned that the latter are almost as different from Prussians as chalk is from cheese. The Rhinelander understands better than any other German how to be *gemüthlich*. He lives in a land of sun and vineyards and, although he tills his fields and his wife bakes and scours with as much vigor as any other *Hausfrau,* it is clear that he does not possess that enormous industry and iron sense of discipline which are so deeply rooted in the character of every true Prussian. Hindenburg, though in every sense a true Prussian, fully understood the necessity of relaxation and the importance of devoting a certain amount of leisure to the enjoyment of life. In Hindenburg's youth outdoor games and sports, as they have so long been understood and practised in England, were almost unknown in Germany. The present enthusiasm for sport is entirely a post-war development, and there can be little doubt that it is greatly improving the spirit of the present-day German youth. Hindenburg, however, rode and shot and was no damper on any kind of pleasure. The men of the Rhine country did not therefore find him uncongenial: indeed, he was captivated by their joyful way of living and spent many happy hours by the shores of the River Rhine. His commanding general here was at first General Vogel von Falckenstein, who had been his departmental chief in the Ministry for War, but, shortly after Hindenburg's appointment to the 4th Army Corps, Falckenstein was replaced by the heir to the Grand Duchy of Baden. Hindenburg speaks of the three and a half years which followed as among the happiest of his life. His chief, who united great ability and devotion to duty with unusual charm of manner and with a sympathy which endeared him to everyone, became Hindenburg's close friend. Again, however, he was due for transfer, and in 1900 he was appointed commander of the 28th Division at Karlsruhe. Here he and his wife were warmly received and made much of by the Grand Duke and Duchess of Baden, whose court was at Karlsruhe.

In the 28th Division, infantry, cavalry and artillery were united under one command, and the divisional commander was therefore in a position to acquire a detailed as well as a general view of the employment of those branches in war. One or two stories have been told of the tests which Hindenburg applied to the soldiers in order to see whether they were really awake to the importance of details. Among other matters stressed was the importance of recognizing the rank of an officer by his badges. The non-commissioned officers, therefore, taught all the recruits the meaning of the

PRESIDENT VON HINDENBURG AS MAJOR GENERAL AND
CHIEF OF THE GENERAL STAFF OF THE EIGHTH ARMY CORPS
IN 1897 AT COBLENTZ

different signs, and the new men were also usually told of Hindenburg's enormous moustache that they might more easily recognize him. A day of inspection came and Hindenburg appeared. The inspection over, as usual, he started to put questions. Addressing an honest Pomeranian, he said: "Now, my son, how, for example, would you recognize the commander of your division?" To the astonished horror of all the officers, the young man replied without hesitation, *"Am Schnautz!"* [1] On another occasion, Hindenburg, who was painfully exact and punctual, asked a recruit what the length of a period of ten minutes was. "Why, ten minutes!" replied the boy. Hindenburg, however, wished to make a test, took his watch from his pocket, and said: "Now I shall look at my watch, and you must tell me when you think the ten minutes have passed." The recruit stood at attention, and, at the end of five minutes, Hindenburg asked whether ten had gone by. "No," said the recruit. But, when precisely ten minutes were over, the soldier shouted "Halt!" and the much-feared Divisional Commander was full of praise for this clever young man. Finally he asked him how he was able to judge time with such accuracy. Pat came the reply, "By the tower clock over there!"

This period spent at Karlsruhe served to strengthen Hindenburg's understanding of the south German temperament. He found the people of Baden genial and kindly, and his connection with them was of the pleasantest. The Grand Duke and Duchess offered him constant hospitality, doubtless pleased to entertain the general who for so long had served with their son and had stood so high in his regard.

[1] "By the snout!"

But the Karlsruhe days were not to pass without sorrow, for, in 1902, nine years after the death of his wife, von Hindenburg's father followed her to the grave at the mature age of eighty-six. He was buried in the black cloak of the Order of St. John under the shadow of a lime tree in the cemetery at Neudeck. He had lived just long enough to see his son promoted lieutenant-general.

Hindenburg left Karlsruhe and his division in 1903 to take over the command of the 4th Army Corps at Magdeburg. He accepted with joy the heavy responsibilities involved in such a command. He delighted to pick out and remedy the weak spots that came under his notice and to make each man feel that he was equal to his task. Over the young officers attached to his staff he exercised a boundless influence. When reproof was necessary he never indulged in cheap sarcasm, but stated his displeasure in a few short sentences which impressed the culprit but did not make him feel hurt or sullen. In his senior cadet days, when occasion arose for him to point out to a junior the error of his ways, he frequently concluded his remarks with the observation: "Remember—you want to become an officer!" To be an officer, so far as Hindenburg was concerned, meant to be a man who did his job efficiently, quietly, and with a definite enthusiasm for the task in hand. His own thoroughness was a by-word, and in view of his tireless example it was not possible for a young officer under his command to do anything but his best.

Magdeburg, where Hindenburg was now quartered, is not an especially interesting town, though it has its "old part" and its fine cathedral. Nor is it especially beautiful, but large and carefully planted parks supply, to some extent,

the deficiencies of nature. Hindenburg, with his happy gift
of adapting himself to any society, soon felt at home there.
It is worthy of mention that a Foundation for the support
of veterans of 1870 existed in the town; the donations to
the Fund were distributed to the old soldiers yearly, on the
Kaiser's birthday, and this was also always the occasion of
a little celebration. Hindenburg, in consequence of his
manifold duties, was generally somewhat inaccessible. The
chairman of the Foundation once sent a message to know
when he could speak to him. "When it is a case of the
old veterans, you can come and see me at any time," was
the reply, "and you need not rig yourself up for the occasion
—just come along as you are."

At Magdeburg, he came in touch with all ranks and professions, and he was quick to recognize worth and merit
wherever he encountered it, for he was never guilty of that
narrowness, common among the pre-war German officers,
which would blind men to the value of any calling other
than that of a soldier. He did not indulge in snobbery and
patronage, and he welcomed many types of people as guests
in his house.

The immediate world around Hindenburg saw only a
soldier who understood his duty and pursued it relentlessly,
but his friends and guests were allowed to see something of
the intimate life of his family. Some of its charm is revealed
in the following letters written to his son.

Madgeburg, January 31, 1905.

MY DEAR BOY:

Today my thoughts, wishes and prayers are much with you, the
more so as you are unfortunately ill. Take good care of yourself
and come here as soon as you can, so that we can nurse you up
and you can improve your health and convalesce. Be sure to take

a closed carriage from the barracks to the Potsdam station, so that you don't catch cold. I suppose you will let us know the day and hour of your arrival either by letter or telegraphically.

But it has pleased me very much that you remained at your post to the last, and that you duly paraded our recruits. That is how a Prussian officer must behave.

Now, for today, God bless you, my dear child. May we meet soon!

With fond love,

YOUR OLD FATHER.

MY DEAR CHILD:

Our thoughts and best wishes are with you today, my old boy. God bless you! Only do be very careful and come to us as soon as possible. Your mother's greeting from the store-cupboard will probably be too much for you to deal with yourself—perhaps your comrades will help you along.

With truest love,

YOUR MOTHER.

Magdeburg, February 4, 1909.

MY DEAR SON:

I am delighted that you are to be made adjutant. I know that you will prove worthy of the trust thus placed on you, and then this time will have its influence on your whole military future. The post of adjutant demands not only industry, thoroughness and reliability in the saddle and at the writing-desk, but, what is just as important, a proper tact. One is not there to put oneself on a high horse so far as the troop is concerned, but to ease its existence, and to form a connecting member between it and the commander. And, so far as the latter is concerned, one must always remember that he is the superior and that he is a much older and more practical soldier. One has to apply his decisions and not to try and force one's own upon him. If he now and then permits suggestions owing to a trust in you, which must first be won, these must always be made in the most modest manner; and the troop must never be allowed to think that the adjutant "does the job." If that should happen, the adjutant is no good. . . . I am glad your new horse pleases you. . . .

YOUR OLD FATHER.

All good wishes, my dear child. I am sorry that you cannot come to us for Maundy Thursday, and go with us to Holy Communion. Last year you couldn't either—or we could not because of Ann's illness—but if it is at all possible, go to Holy Communion on Maundy Thursday or Good Friday with some of your comrades, that is, if you should not after all manage to come to us.

A thousand good wishes, my child,

FROM YOUR MOTHER.

Magdeburg, 29. 1. 11.

MY DEAR BOY:

The best of all good wishes for your birthday. Remain well content, true to duty and taking pleasure in its fulfilment, and continue to bring your name credit and your parents pleasure. I should be very glad if your wish to go to the *Akademie* could be fulfilled. In that case you would certainly be sent to the artillery and cavalry at Hanover in the summer; that would be very nice. Get thoroughly down to work through February, and then come here for a few days at the beginning of March after the examination. We expect to leave Magdeburg some time after the 20th of March.

Write soon, my dear boy; we always long to hear from you. . . .

YOUR OLD FATHER.

While at Magdeburg, Hindenburg spent much of his leisure shooting. There were plenty of hares and pheasant coverts in Saxony and the owners of neighboring estates preserved deer and all kinds of other game.

But Hindenburg was nearly sixty-five years old and, as he writes in his memoirs: [1]

. . . Little by little the decision grew in me to retire from the army. I had attained far more in my military career than I had ever dared to hope. There was no prospect of war, and so I recognized it was my duty to clear the way for the advancement of younger men, and I asked in 1911 for permission to resign. As this unimportant circumstance has given rise to many legends, I wish

[1] *Aus meinem Leben.*

[39]

to state emphatically that this step was not occasioned by any friction, either from a service or from a personal point of view.

The parting from the 4th Army Corps was very hard, but "it had to be." The town of Hanover, where he had been so happy in his young days, was the place to which he elected to retire.

Hindenburg concerned himself little with politics, but his ideas are expressed in his memoirs.

A firmly self-contained state, according to Bismarck's conception, was the world in which I felt best. Discipline and work within the Fatherland meant more to me than any cosmopolitan dreams. Also I recognized no right for any citizen over against which a duty of equal weight could not be placed.

For Hindenburg, the whole round world was bound not with chains of gold, but with the iron chain of duty. Before everything else he was a good soldier, and his whole-hearted devotion to the task in hand, however distasteful it might be to him, and the complete grasp he therefore acquired of every phase of military life, were later to win him his laurels in his country's bitter hour of need.

Anyone who does not regard our military labors in the time of peace with a prejudiced eye must at least recognize our army as the finest school for the training of will and action and for the joy in doing work. How many thousands of people have learned under its influence to what mental and physical heights they could rise, and have there won self-confidence and that inward strength which then remained theirs for the rest of their lives!

It is very certain that the army discipline and training gave Hindenburg "that inward strength" which enabled him to achieve three gigantic tasks (the winning of the Battle of Tannenberg, the supervision of the return of the German armies to Germany after the War, and the work of President) at a time of life when most men think of rest. Other generals in their old age have fought and won battles, but no other man, after four years of grueling warfare against an ever-increasing enemy, has had to conduct the return of a defeated and starving soldiery into a starving and revolutionary country. It might well have been expected that a man who had negotiated such difficulties would beg to be left to finish his days in peace and quiet; but, when, in his ripe old age, another arduous duty was offered to him, the old soldier, who had never listened to any voice but that of duty, once again obeyed its call and accepted the high, difficult office of the presidency.

In the meantime, he lived at Hanover, enjoying a well-earned leisure, and following his son's career with the closest attention and pride. At this time, too, he studied politics, but his observations were not reassuring. He studied also the troubles of the Balkan states; letters to his son, written in October, 1912, evidence keen interest in their struggles. They reveal also an absolute understanding of the military situations involved and an unerring recognition of any weak spot in tactics.

Apart from his interest in the outside world, he was able to enjoy a quiet, agreeable family life. His daughters had both married and gone to homes of their own. The peaceful hours and days lengthened into years, season followed season, until, one summer day, the telegraph wires flashed to the countries of the world that message which told of the murder of the heir to the throne of Austria and his wife.

CHAPTER IV

THE news of the Archduke's death reached the Kaiser at Kiel, and he returned at once to Berlin, with the intention of proceeding to Vienna for the funeral. The journey, however, was not undertaken because there seemed to be no assurance that his person would be safe.

Events moved swiftly. The Austrian government, having secured a friendly note from Germany, prepared the demands to be made upon Serbia. In Russia, England and Italy there was considerable anxiety with regard to Austria's plans. The anxiety spread to Berlin, and, on July 20, the German minister in Vienna made an urgent demand that the precise wording of the ultimatum to Serbia be communicated to him. The required information reached Berlin on the evening of July 22, that is to say, at a time when it was not possible for anything to be done. The fatal document, which had been despatched to Belgrade on the 20th, was so worded as to make war inevitable. The brand had been lighted, and it remained only to be seen how far the blaze would spread.

In the meantime the attitude of Italy was regarded with mistrust in both Berlin and Vienna, and the reports from the German embassy in Rome soon showed that the Italians were not disposed to sit and look on quietly at a war between Austria and Serbia. Berchtold,[1] who had preserved the

[1] Foreign Secretary for Austria.

utmost secrecy with regard to his procedure, had awakened suspicion in high circles in Rome, where it was believed that this secrecy denoted an Austrian threat to Italian interests in the Balkans. Rome made it plain to the German ambassador that neither Italy nor Roumania would tolerate the overthrow of Serbia, or even an annexation of Serbian territory by Austria. Berchtold, at first disinclined to come to a clear understanding with Italy, finally yielded to the pressure of Germany, and disavowed any intent to acquire Serbian territory. On the 28th and 29th of July, Lichnowsky's reports instructed Berlin as to the way matters stood in Italy, and from Vienna came the news that Italy was in agreement with the measures Austria proposed to adopt. The cabinet in Vienna, in fact, gave its anti-Serbian actions different guises in Berlin, Rome, London and St. Petersburg, and the lighted brand was flaring dangerously.

On July 30, the German chancellor gave the Prussian ministers an outline of the position. He characterized the Italian attitude as "not quite transparent." The dispute between Austria and Serbia was there regarded with apprehension because Italian interests in the Balkans seemed to be threatened.

On July 31, Italy roundly stated that the demeanor of Austria towards Serbia was "aggressive," and the old enmity towards Austria grew more intense with each passing hour, helped, to no little extent, by the secretive, blundering methods of Berchtold. And there is no doubt that this minister was greatly to blame for Italy's withdrawal from her alliance with Germany and Austria.

Russia did not, in the early days, evince any hesitation.

She ranged herself immediately and openly on the side of Serbia, and violent and unbridled newspaper articles inflamed the whole country against the Central European powers. The German ambassador did what he could to convince the Russian ministers that severe measures must be adopted against Serbia, but he spoke to ears that were entirely prejudiced, and as early as on July 6 news had penetrated to Berlin that Russia was preparing for war. And what could an embassy hope to achieve in a country where the clang of arms was already to be heard and where a belligerent press was stridently acclaiming war? In addition, the German ambassador had to contend with a minister [1] whose implacable hatred for Austria formed an insurmountable barrier to reasonable negotiation. A lurid light now shone in the sky, and the war clouds gathered.

And France? In the middle of July Germany cherished at least some hope that France would not interfere, as is revealed in a letter, dated July 16, from the German chancellor to Graf Noerdern, the secretary of state for Alsace-Lorraine. He wrote: "We have grounds for assuming, and we are bound to hope, that France, burdened as she now is with all kinds of difficulties, will do all she can to restrain Russia from interference. . . . If we could only succeed now, not only in keeping France quiet, but in getting her to force Russia to keep the peace, this should have a reaction most favorable for us upon the Franco-Russian alliance." France gave no positive indication of her attitude in the first days after the murder. But Poincaré and Viviani were in St. Petersburg between the 20th and the 23rd of

[1] Sazonov.

July on official business, and there they came to an agreement with the Russian ministers to intervene in Serbia's favor in Vienna and to invite England to join them in this step.

But, thanks to her insular position, England seemed for the moment aloof from the atmosphere of threat and storm. All the nations of Europe watched anxiously to see what she would say. Public opinion there demanded that the murderer be punished, but it was soon made plain that England, also, would object to any change in the then-existing Balkan conditions. Austria should be satisfied, of course, and the English ambassador in St. Petersburg went to work according to his instructions. On July 18 he reported that Austria's ultimatum to Serbia would not be quietly accepted in Russia. Lord Grey, on July 20, informed the German ambassador that a war between the great European powers was unthinkable and must be stopped at all costs. On the 22nd, Lichnowsky was able to inform Berlin that the British cabinet would move in the matter of the acceptance of the Austrian note to Belgrade, provided it was of a proper nature and could be reconciled with Serbian independence. That England would take part in any war which might break out, even should France and Russia be drawn into it, found little credence in Berlin official circles, and none at all in the German nation as a whole.

On July 23, the Austrian ambassador to Serbia handed his government's note in at Belgrade. The violent, immoderate nature of its contents could be excused to a certain extent by the crime which had caused the words to be written. The answer was to be given at the latest on July 25, at six o'clock in the evening, and it was received by the Austrian government a few minutes before that time. All the world knows what the result of that answer was. The Serbian ambassador left Vienna on the same evening, and the Austrian ambassadorial staff received orders to quit Belgrade. Diplomatic relations having been broken off, the command for the mobilization of the Serbian army was immediately given. The bugles began to call and the flags to fly and the first hysteria began.

Weeks had been wasted in Vienna in settling the terms in which the note to Serbia was to be couched, and the first outburst of horror at the murder and sympathy with the Austrian court had died down. Had Austria been guided by a powerful and decisive statesman to demand instant punishment of the murderer and due reparation, his action would have been supported by the righteous indignation of the whole continent. But Berchtold adopted a shilly-shallying policy and did not even reveal his intentions in Berlin until it was too late for anything to be done to improve the situation. And Germany had given her approval to the proceedings of the Austrian government.

On July 21, Germany had sought to justify Austria in London, Paris and St. Petersburg. The ambassadors were instructed to impress upon the foreign powers that Germany desired a "strict localization of any war that might break out." But Austria's ultimatum to Serbia made the worst impression possible, and the German explanations of July 24 in Paris, London and St. Petersburg were unable to eradicate or even to diminish it. Suggestions from London that Serbia should be given more time fell on deaf ears.

Although Austria was really determined on war, Berchtold wished to reassure Russia to a certain extent, and to that end Graf Szapáry informed Sazonov on July 25 that Austria had no intention of laying hands on the sovereignty of Serbia and had no wish to annex territory from her; and, on July 27, a further assurance was added that no one in Austria wished to threaten Russian interests. But, as Austria refused to discuss the text of the notes, Sazonov's easily aroused suspicions leaped to openly expressed distrust, and negotiations were broken off. At the instance of Germany, there was one more fruitless attempt to renew them on July 30.

On the 29th of July, Lichnowsky gave Berlin an account of a conversation with Lord Grey, in which the latter expressed himself clearly with regard to England's policy in the event of a European war's breaking out. His remarks were not given the serious consideration that they merited. Neither the Kaiser nor his advisers thought it likely that England would do other than remain neutral.

On July 30 Grey sent a note to Austria, begging her to be content with the occupation of Belgrade or some part of Serbia until the powers should succeed in settling the differences with Russia; and during the course of the 30th and 31st, the British representative in Vienna came repeatedly to the authorities for their reply. No answer, however, was forthcoming, and it was only on August 1 that Berchtold expressed his willingness to discuss the matter. But against this reply must be set an already fixed determination on the part of Austria not to refrain, in any circumstances, from war measures against Serbia. It might have been possible to reach an understanding, but at the last moment the news came of the general mobilization of the Russian army.

Austria intended to send a force of eight army corps against Serbia; and Russia, immediately after the Austrian declaration of war on Serbia, sent thirteen army corps against Austria. On the same day, July 29, the call for general mobilization of the Russian army was sent out. In Berlin, where this news was followed by information regarding French preparations for war, anxiety became acute, although the Russians sent to say that their operations were not in the least directed against Germany. It could not be concealed, however, that preparations for war were also proceeding apace in the northwestern part of Russia. The German ambassador was instructed to repeat his warnings to Sazonov. The latter construed the warning as a threat, and as such it was reported in Paris and in London.

On the 1st of August, at five o'clock, the German declaration of war against Russia was made. For economic reasons, apart from any questions of treaties, France was forced to side with Russia in order to protect her solvency. As soon as news of Russian war measures reached Paris, France started her military preparations. The German ambassador was accordingly instructed to ask whether France would remain neutral in a war between Russia and Germany. The answer, given on August 1, was that France would "do what was demanded by her interests." A few hours after this rather ambiguous reply, the order was given for mobilization of the army and navy. In the meantime, the newspapers did not neglect their opportunities, and, referring to the War of 1870, they fanned public opinion and patriotic hysteria to fever heat. On the 3rd of August Germany declared war on France.

England still held back, but on the night of August 3 German troops crossed the boundary of Belgium, and on August 4 England declared war on Germany. The German parliament sought to justify this violation of the Belgian neutrality by stating that the measure was demanded by the exigencies of the moment, and that the country would be compensated, fully and properly, for all damage. On August 11 France declared war on Austria, and England's declaration against Austria followed on the 13th. Japan, having demanded unconditional withdrawal of the Germans from Kiaochow—a demand which remained unanswered—declared war on August 23.

Little by little, other declarations followed until, finally, all the powers in the world were engaged in this unprecedented struggle. The brand had done its work and the guns began to speak.

In a large, comfortable house in the town of Hanover, a retired general watched the development of the situation with the utmost closeness. Did he—that iron martinet, who knew so thoroughly everything that could be achieved with an army of first-class quality—ever remember in those hours that he had once called war "the normal condition for a soldier"? He was older now, and wiser, and perhaps it was rather the words which his father had once written to his mother that came into his mind:

"O God, what a rod of punishment in Thy hand is this torch of war!"

CHAPTER V

EVERY man, woman and child in Germany was gripped immediately by the excitement in the air. Perhaps for the first time in history, the many states which composed the empire were united in one common feeling. The war had come, and now only the soldiers counted. Every man who wore a uniform was a hero and walked surrounded by a golden haze of romance.

Hindenburg waited in his house at Hanover for his call to arms. He watched the magnificent German armies moving off to the fronts. Of these he justly writes: "a magnificent power, whose equal the world has seldom seen." And still he waited. All the soldier in him had re-awakened, and he was conscious that he knew more of tactics and more about the eastern defence of his country than most other generals; but he did not know whether he would be called upon to use his knowledge. It seemed to him that there were plenty of younger men who would come first. He waited.

All German eyes were turned to the fronts, and the first news which reached the waiting crowds was good. The fall of Liège, the successful result of the battle at Mülhausen, the irresistible onward sweep of the armies through Belgium were acclaimed and celebrated. Even from the east came no threatening tidings.

At last the anxiously awaited telegram was delivered to von Hindenburg at three o'clock in the afternoon. It contained an inquiry from the Kaiser as to whether the general was prepared for immediate employment. His reply, "Am ready," had hardly been despatched when he received a second telegram from headquarters. This informed him that General Ludendorff would arrive in Hanover at three o'clock the following morning; and it was followed by a third message appointing Hindenburg commander of the Army in the East. Preparations followed.

Towards three o'clock in the morning, Hindenburg drove to the station to await the special train in which Ludendorff was being hurried to Hanover. He had been hastily recalled from the western front to Coblenz and personally instructed by Moltke. The situation in East Prussia had become suddenly intensely serious, for the Commander of the 8th Army [1] had seen fit to cut short activities after the victorious battle at Gumbinnen because he had news of the approach towards the south boundary of Prussia of an overwhelming Russian force, and he thought that the only possible chance to stem the enemy's tide was to evacuate the whole of East Prussia. At General Headquarters it was hastily decided that a change of leadership in the East was imperative, and the leadership of the army was placed in Hindenburg's hands, while Ludendorff was appointed chief officer of the General Staff of the 8th Army.

Hindenburg and Ludendorff, who did not know each other, met at about four o'clock in the morning of August 23. In his memoirs, Hindenburg states that only at the moment

[1] General von Prittwitz.

when the train drove into the station was he able to tear his thoughts completely away from the home he had left in such a hurry. Ludendorff immediately explained the position in the east to Hindenburg, according to von Moitke's instructions. Since then, the army, supported by garrisons from fortresses and certain companies of the militia, had moved into positions in preparation for the defence of the southern frontier of West and East Prussia from the Vistula to the lake district near Lötzen. The army had met the Russians on the 17th of August at Stallupönen, and on the 19th and 20th at Gumbinnen. Here the battle had been broken off owing to the threat to the German rear and flank from the Russian approach to the southern boundary line. The High Command of the Eastern Army, having thus cut short the action at Gumbinnen, reported to General Headquarters that they were no longer in a position to hold the country east of the Vistula. Ludendorff further delivered the Kaiser's order that the Russians were to be attacked, and reported that he (Ludendorff) had given certain urgent orders from Coblenz to ensure that operations should go forward on the territory east of the Vistula. Moltke had strongly disapproved the suggestion of evacuation.

The union of Hindenburg and Ludendorff became very close. Much has been written about their respective abilities, and attempts have been made to give the glory for their achievements solely to one or to the other. It seems, however, that to Hindenburg, without doubt, belonged the ideas and the tactical methods employed, while Ludendorff accepted the whole responsibility for their execution. Hindenburg had the vision and grasp of the situation and saw with clear eyes what the situation demanded. It was, however, the dynamic personality of Ludendorff and his untiring energy that carried out the ideas of the master tactician. In his book, "Hindenburg," the French general Buat compares the memoirs which Hindenburg and Ludendorff published and observes that, whereas Hindenburg practically always uses the pronoun "we," Ludendorff's book is characterized by a constantly recurring use of the word "I." Buat's final judgment of the combination of these two men is expressed in the words:—

That the latter [Ludendorff] was the arm, is certain; that in some cases, and not always the happiest, he was also the head is beyond doubt. But, if the field marshal often permitted himself to approve suggestions, he never did so without complete awareness of what he did, for he had great insight. It is only relatively that one may accuse him of a certain weakness of character; for Ludendorff possessed a stronger will, the will of a fanatic, which drives straight to its goal without any consideration of obstacles or people who may be in the way. In the marriage effected on August 23, 1914, the first quartermaster-general was the dominating husband.

At least there is no doubt that Hindenburg and Ludendorff were well suited to one another, and it is certain that Hindenburg's assured and matured judgments and the range of his vision in matters military secured the respect of "the dominating husband" and possibly restrained his irritable and less perfectly balanced temper.

Their conversation at this first meeting did not occupy more than half an hour, at the end of which time they parted to snatch some sleep.

"So," writes Hindenburg, "we went to meet a common

future, fully conscious of its seriousness, but also full of firm trust in God, in our gallant troops and, not least, in each other. Common thoughts and common deeds were now to unite us over a period of years."

On August 23, early in the afternoon, the two generals reached Marienburg, which was their headquarters. As Marienburg lies to the east of the Vistula, they were already in the field of action. Hindenburg made an immediate study of recent developments. The 20th Army Corps had moved eastwards from its frontier station at Neidenburg, and the 3rd Reserve Division, supporting the 20th Army Corps, had arrived at Allenstein. The 1st Army Corps, which had been ordered to Deutsch Eylau, had been delayed; but the 17th Army Corps and the 1st Reserves had arrived on foot in the neighborhood of Gerdauen. A Russian cavalry corps was reported to be at Angerburg, and another at Darkehman. One division of Samsonov's army had apparently reached Ortelsburg, and it was reported that Johannisburg was already in the hands of the enemy.

The pocketbook of a fallen Russian officer yielded up a piece of paper from which the intentions of the enemy could be ascertained—plans for a concentrated attack upon the German 8th Army. The Russian army of Rennenkampf, consisting of 246,000 men and 800 guns, had been in action against the Germans at Gumbinnen. The 2nd Russian Army, which was approaching from the south under Samsonov, consisted of 289,000 men and 780 guns. Against these forces, the Germans had 210,000 men and 600 guns, numbers which had been, of course, reduced by the actions [1] in which a part of the army had already been engaged.

[1] Stallupönen and Gumbinnen.

Obviously, the only chance for the Germans was to defeat Samsonov utterly and then to drive Rennenkampf's army away from East Prussia where it was bringing plunder, murder and ruin in its train. Hindenburg's plan was uncomplicated but very bold, and it was dependent for its success upon the morale of the German soldiers. However, as he himself says, a man at whose back lie his home, his wife and children and all he holds dear, fights more determinedly to prevent a ruthless foe from gaining access to them, and the men in this army were Prussians, "children of the threatened province." Against Samsonov's front, therefore, Hindenburg placed a thin line of soldiers which might "give to the pressure of the opposing masses, if only it did not break," and while this line faced the Russian hosts, two strong detachments were to make decisive attacks from right and left. The 1st Army Corps, supported by militia, were brought in from the northwest, and the 17th Army Corps and 1st Reserve Corps with a brigade of militia were brought from the north and the northeast. Hindenburg realized that complete annihilation of his opponents represented the only chance to save Prussia from further ghastly ravages, and he never for an instant forgot the fight between Russia and Austria-Hungary that was being waged in Galicia and Poland. "Should our first blow not be final," he wrote,[1] "then the danger to our homes would remain like a gnawing disease, the murder and burnings in East Prussia would go unrevenged and our ally[2] in the south would wait in vain for our assistance."

Against Rennenkampf, lying in the northeast, a division of cavalry, some reserves and two militia reserves were

[1] *Aus meinem Leben.*   [2] Austria.

placed. Hindenburg hoped that Rennenkampf would be deceived as to the strength against him and that, at least, the little army would serve to cover the operations of the forces attacking Samsonov. It was also a question whether Rennenkampf would not come to the help of Samsonov by falling upon the Germans from the rear, for the little force left over against his positions would be powerless to prevent this development, even though they might be strengthened by the addition of two militia brigades, which were even then en route from Schleswig-Holstein.

On August 24, Hindenburg traveled to the headquarters of the 20th Army Corps at Tannenberg, the spot where the Slavs had triumphed over the Germans more than five centuries before, and where now was to come so signal a reversal of the situation. On the same day the German soldiers started on their march to outflank the enemy. The roads were full of refugees who, with what goods they could carry, were trying to make for safety. These straying numbers on the roads prevented the easy movement of the army. It was reckoned that the time required to surround the Russians would be two days, so that manœuvre could not become effective till the 26th. Until then, the thin centre line of the front had to hold on. In places, this line gave and was forced back on to the left wing, driven to bend by the shattering fire and overwhelming numbers of the enemy. It bent, but it did not break. Hindenburg's boundless trust in his soldiers was not in vain. In the meantime his glance was anxious, for it seemed possible that the Russians would extend over Lautenburg and destroy the flanking movement. News was also received that Rennenkampf was on the march, but he was moving slowly and westwards towards Königsberg. It looked almost as if the Russians had given up their original plans or else were deceived as to where the real strength of the German Army lay.

The 26th of August saw the beginning of the terrible struggle which stretched from Lautenburg to a spot north of Bischofsburg. The battle was fought in groups along a front of about seventy-five miles, and it occurred "in a series of attacks and not in one concerted action."

The right wing, under General von François, made its advance towards Uzdowo.

The struggle at Bischofsburg was grim; the German soldiers, though far outnumbered, fought doggedly through the evening hours.

The right wing of Samsonov's army was severely beaten by the German 17th Army Corps and 1st Reserve Corps, supported by militia, and was forced to retire to Ortelsburg.

So far, so good. But headquarters awaited with great anxiety what the next day would bring forth. It was sure that the Russians would offer a further strong resistance. Disquieting reports arrived. One of Rennenkampf's corps was moving through Angerburg, and the question arose: Would not his corps attack from the rear the German left-wing attacking party? Further, the flank and rear of the German west wing was menaced by a strong detachment of Russian cavalry. It seemed not unlikely that this was supported by infantry.

"The battle," writes Hindenburg, "had reached its crisis. The question forced its way into our minds: How will the situation develop if . . . the decision should be delayed for several days? Is it surprising that heavy thoughts are in many hearts, that fixed determination threatens to give way to hesitation, that distraction makes itself felt where previously only clear ideas held sway? Ought not we, after all, to strengthen our force against Rennenkampf even though we should weaken our attack on Samsonov? Would it not be better to refrain from attempting to destroy the Narew army in order to make sure that we ourselves are not annihilated? We overcame this vacillation, remained true to our first decision, and again pressed with all our strength for a solution."

Accordingly, the order was given which commanded the Germans to approach the enemy at four o'clock in the morning and to "act with the greatest energy." The 27th of August was a great day. The enemy retreated and finally fled from the battlefields. The threat from Rennenkampf's forces, it proved, existed "only in the imagination of an airman." In reality, Rennenkampf was still marching upon the strong fortress of Königsberg, where he probably still thought the full force of the German defences lay. Samsonov's right wing was broken and routed; the danger to his left wing grew hourly more and more certain. On the same day François and Scholtz were successful in their attacks upon the enemy posts at Uzdowo. The Russians might now advance upon Allenstein (the centre front) as they wished. It would end in their ruin, for the order was now given to surround the central force of their army, their 13th and 15th Army Corps. All day, on the 28th, the savage fight continued. The Russian losses were appalling, and the German sufficiently heavy for the small army. Desperate resistance was offered, but it was in vain, and, on the 29th, the principal portion of the Russian army was finally and utterly defeated at Hohenstein. And through all these days Rennenkampf, completely deceived by Hindenburg's amazing strategy, continued his peaceful descent upon Königsberg. While his comrade was being defeated by a far smaller force, he wasted those hours and days in futile inaction, and this was the general who, of all Russian military leaders, had the greatest name.

A few German troops were withdrawn from the battle, so that they might cover, in case of need, the terrible final stages. Long columns of prisoners appeared, tattered, worn out, and many wounded. The files grew and grew to an almost incredible extent. Hindenburg had occasion to notice here how the Prussian soldiers almost immediately lost their animosity, and in how humane a manner they treated the prisoners. Their hatred, however, against the Cossacks was scarcely to be restrained, and it frequently chanced that these tore the stripes from their trousers to avoid recognition. It must not be inferred that any Prussian soldier so forgot his rigid training and discipline as to torture the prisoners, but it is certain that they were roughly handled by men who had seen the devastation wrought by the invaders, had seen German homes burned, and who knew of other unspeakable atrocities committed against non-combatants by this half-savage soldiery. The very fact that the Cossacks tried to conceal their identity by the mutilation of their uniforms goes to show, at least, that some consciousness of guilt existed among them.

On August 30, the Russians attacked from east and south

in an endeavor to break through the surrounding Germans and to release their comrades from the circle fast narrowing around them. From Myszyniec and from Ostroleka came these strong, fresh troops, marching against the backs of the Germans. Other Russian columns of considerable strength were reported to be moving. But Hindenburg held to his plans, which had so far been successful. Reserves were sent against the new hosts. Closer and closer swept the German encirclement, and the imprisoned Russians sought their escape now this way and now that, but in vain. The grueling fire to which they were subjected gave them no chance. From the direction of Laudsberg, the Rennenkampf cavalry was approaching the field of Tannenberg, but at Allenstein a strong force of German soldiers had been mustered. These men were tired from the days of desperate fighting through which they had passed, but they had all the consciousness of their marvelous victory to support them. There was not a man who was not ready to do his utmost, and more than his utmost if need be, to ensure that their triumph might not be wrenched away. The 31st of August saw the retreat of Rennenkampf upon Allenburg and Angerburg, and the close of the day saw the final collapse of Samsonov's army. The battle of Tannenberg was won, and Hindenburg was able to send the Kaiser his report on the work done.

I humbly beg to report to your Majesty that the struggle with the greatest part of the Russian Army is finished. The 13th, 15th and 18th Army Corps have been annihilated. Up to the present, there are over 60,000 prisoners, including the generals commanding the 13th and 15th Army Corps. The guns are still in the woods and are being collected. The spoils, which are extraordinarily great, cannot at the present time be detailed. The corps which were outside the central struggle (the 1st and 6th) have also suffered heavily and are in flight through Mlawa and Myszyniec.

The results of that terrific task were flashed in those few, dry words to the Kaiser, and the name of their sender became, in one moment, a household word throughout his country. Like Byron, he had become famous in a day, for, outside military circles, he had been entirely unknown. The Kaiser conferred upon him the order Pour le Mérite. And Hindenburg?

"In Allenstein, our new military headquarters, I went during the service to the church in the neighborhood of the old castle. As the priest pronounced the benediction all those present, young soldiers and old *Landstürmer*,[1] sank to their knees, under the immense impression left on them by their past experiences. A worthy conclusion to their deeds of heroism."

[1] Territorials.

CHAPTER VI

ON August 31, the High Command of the 8th Army received a telegram stating that the 11th Army Corps, a reserve corps of guards and the 8th Cavalry Division were being conveyed to the eastern front. Such reserves as could be spared were ordered to pursue the beaten Russian Army and also to clear the eastern frontier of Rennenkampf's army. The telegram concluded by stating that, should the position in East Prussia permit of such a step, the 8th Army should then proceed in the direction of Warsaw. The telegram meant that the plan of war agreed upon between Germany and Austria-Hungary was to be executed if this were possible. This plan was simply that the Austrian forces should advance in strength and attack the eastern part of Russian Poland, while the German army crossed over the Narew from East Prussia to meet them. But concerning this plan Hindenburg was to write:—

A great and fine idea; but, in the present position, it had considerable weakness. It did not take into account the fact that Austria-Hungary would send a strong army to the Serbian frontier; nor the fact that Russia would be able to stand fully equipped on the frontier a few weeks after the outbreak of hostilities; or the fact that 800,000 men would be sent against East Prussia; and, least of all, the fact that this plan had already been betrayed to the Russian General Staff before the war began.

Such was the situation with which Hindenburg was faced. Rennenkampf's strong force was still in its positions, and

Austria was engaged in a bitter struggle of which the issue was doubtful. It was obvious, however, that Prussia must first be freed from Rennenkampf's army before the Germans could undertake a southward march to the aid of her ally.

Rennenkampf's men were drawn up along a line stretching from the Deime, through Allenburg, Gerdauen and Angerburg. Hindenburg was uninformed of what might lie in the district southeast of the Masurian Lakes. There was strong suspicion that Grajewo and its neighborhood were occupied by Russians. Some considerable activity was observed in the district to the rear of Rennenkampf's army, and there seemed to be advances towards the southwest and the west. There was no doubt that Rennenkampf was being reinforced, for his communications were excellent. The Russian leader dealt with a degree of indecision and lack of energy that seems now almost incredible. With more than twenty divisions of infantry at his disposal, he simply stood still, and continued to stand still while the German reinforcements were being brought along as fast as wheels could carry them. Hindenburg writes that "the military calling has habitually, and surprisingly quickly, worn out even strong characters. Where, one year, active ability and driving force have existed, the next year can reveal an unfruitful mind and a faint heart. This has often been the tragedy of great military men."

The absolute defeat of Samsonov had served to show Rennenkampf that the full strength of the German army did not lie in Königsberg, as he had thought. He probably still suspected that no small force occupied the fortress, and it seemed to him safer to lie between the Kurisches Haff and the

Masurian Lakes, in his well-strengthened positions. If he remained where he was, it was almost impossible for the Germans to repeat the tactics of Tannenberg. From the north nothing could be attempted; from the south such manœuvres would be attended with the greatest difficulty. Should the Russian arms win little success or none, they would fall back upon Russia. It was, at any rate, questionable whether the Germans could repeat their success against Samsonov; and, as Samsonov was defeated in attacking, Rennenkampf lay passively where he was. His lack of energy and decision cost him the battle. Against him was a leader who had both the courage and the purpose to carry out his ideas, and under him were Prussian soldiers capable of battling to the last ounce of their strength, soldiers for whom war appeared indeed to be "a normal condition." The position which Hindenburg now had to consider is best explained by himself. He writes:

The great superiority in numbers of the Rennenkampf army was sufficient to enable him to destroy even our strengthened 8th Army. But a premature withdrawal on his part would rob us of the fruits of our new operations and would make it impossible for us to press on to Warsaw in reasonable time and also prevent us from giving the Austrians immediate support. We had, therefore, to be both careful and enterprising.

By September 5 the German armies were in their positions, along a front stretching from Willenberg to Königsberg. The 10th and 11th, the 1st Reserve and Guard Reserve Corps were then sent with the troops from Königsberg against the enemy front. The 1st and 18th Corps were ordered to press through the lake district, and the 3rd Reserve Division was ordered to follow round south of the lake district. Two cavalry divisions were held in readiness to charge forward as soon as the narrow ways through the lakes had been opened up for them. The German leader had spread a strength of fourteen infantry divisions over a front of more than one hundred miles. On the 6th and 7th of September, as the German troops approached the Russian defences, it was possible to see something of the situation in general. At Insterburg and Wehlau the forces of the enemy were heavily massed. Hindenburg suspected that there were even stronger troops to the north of Nordenburg. They remained inactive, however. The 7th of September saw the 3rd Reserve Division's great victory at Bialla, in which about half the Russian 22d Corps was practically destroyed, and the 1st and 17th Corps began to break through the lake district. It was hardly conceivable that Rennenkampf should delay more than twenty-four hours or so longer without showing whether he intended to fight or to retire. Hindenburg watched developments with an anxious heart. It seemed that three more reserve divisions had reached the battlefield, to increase the already enormous numbers of the Russians.

The 8th of September set all doubts at rest. The fight blazed into action along the whole front. The German frontal attack did not succeed in gaining an inch of ground, but the right wing managed to break through the Russians drawn up east of the Masurian Lakes and to turn to the north and the northeast. These troops were trying to reach the Russian communication lines. The cavalry divisions were set in motion, for it seemed that the way to this goal was clear. On the 9th of September the battle raged further, from Angerburg to the Kurisches Haff. Though the German line held, it was unable to advance; but the divisions which had forced their way through to the east of the lakes moved rapidly onwards. The cavalry divisions had, however, to meet an unexpected attack by the enemy and were unable to break this down with the expedition that was required. South of the lakes, the 3rd Reserve Division defeated a greatly superior Russian force at Lyck. From the south, therefore, there was nothing more for Hindenburg to fear. In the north, however, German observation airplanes brought disquieting tidings. Two enemy corps were plainly seen, and a third was being marched to the scene of action near Tilsit. What, wondered Hindenburg, would be the fate of that thin, far-stretched battle line if a determined Russian leader should fall upon it with his vast numbers of men? But it was very far from Rennenkampf's intention to risk an attack. On the night of September 9 the German patrols pressed into the enemy trenches at Gerdauen. They were empty. "The opponent is retiring" was the message sent immediately to Hindenburg and his staff, a message which seemed to them incredible. The 1st Reserve Corps received orders to advance against Insterburg, and to proceed with caution. Midday of September 10 saw the unwelcome news confirmed. Rennenkampf's army was indeed in full retirement, although the Russians were still fighting desperately all along the line. Heavily massed attacks were being launched against the Russians. The right-wing corps and cavalry divisions were directed to the northeast, against the enemy communications, from Insterburg to Kovno.

Covered by their attacking corps, the long columns of Russians withdrew slowly, closely pursued by the Germans.

September 11 was a day of particularly savage fighting, and Insterburg was captured by the Germans. Though it was slow, the Russian retreat was steady, and it would be impossible for the Germans to pursue Rennenkampf across the Niemen. Should the retreat be carried out in safety, then Hindenburg's plans must be regarded as having failed. There were still a few days in which the situation might be retrieved and the Russian army rendered weak and useless. The 3rd Reserve Division reached Suwalki (Russian ground) on September 12. Rennenkampf's southern wing narrowly escaped being surrounded and cut off. The retreat continued, and every passing hour increased the German impatience. It seemed that the men as well as the leaders recognized the urgency of the situation. Hindenburg pays a glowing tribute to the magnificent achievements of some of the pursuers. The men marched and fought, marched and fought, until they dropped to the ground from sheer fatigue. On the 12th of September the headquarters were moved to Insterburg, the former headquarters of Rennenkampf. Long, sullen columns of Russian prisoners were conveyed westward, and the victorious German armies pressed onwards to the east. Hindenburg, in his fastidiousness, shrank somewhat from the occupation of the rooms so recently vacated by the Russian commanders. He speaks scornfully of "remarkable traces of Russian *Halb-Kultur*," [1] and says that the pungent smell of scent did not serve to eradicate other and even less agreeable odors. A smell of perfume in the rooms of a commanding general at the front must certainly have produced a strange impression upon such a man as Hindenburg.

[1] Semi-culture.

Hindenburg relates how exactly one year later he returned through Insterburg from a day's hunting. "At the market-place, my car was turned back because a thanksgiving service was being held there to commemorate the release of the town from Russian occupation. I had to go by another route. *Sic transit gloria mundi!* No one had recognized me."

On the 13th of September, German troops reached Eydt-kuhnen, and directed heavy fire into the retreating Russian hosts. The pursuit had by this time turned the retreat into a rout. The fleeing masses had only one idea—to escape as quickly as possible beyond the wood and marsh country to the west of the line from Olita to Wilewy. They knew that there they would be safe from German pursuit. To prevent annihilation of a large part of his army Rennen-kampf drew up a strong force south of the high road from Virbalis to Vilkaviskis, which the Germans had not suc-ceeded in reaching by the 13th of September. One day only remained to the Germans, after which the Russians would have withdrawn to safety across the swamps. The end of the battle is well known. Thousands of Russians perished miserably in the swamps in their attempt to escape from the fire of the Germans. It was only a shadow of his former force that Rennenkampf was able to lead to safety. In three weeks, the Russians had lost a quarter of a million men and 650 guns, not to mention huge quantities of equipment and stores. East Prussia was cleared, and Hindenburg was hailed as the savior of his country.

In November, 1914, a card was delivered to the field post which bore the address: "To the most popular man in Germany." This was handed, without any hesitation, to Hindenburg. During the fourth month of the war, it was to be seen that the field postman had made no mistake. The shops vied with one another in selling "Hindenburg cigars," "Hindenburg boots," "Hindenburg ties," etc., while the restaurants labeled their best dishes with the name of the great general. The town of Zaborze in Upper Silesia changed its Polish name and became Hindenburg. A schoolmistress in the small town of Königshütte [1] sent a number of letters written by little girls in her class to the victorious leader of the 8th Army. Some of these children, whose ages ranged from eight to ten, expressed their feelings very well indeed, as the following examples show:—

DEAR HERR HINDENBURG:

Thank you very much for being so energetic and for protecting our Fatherland so well. I hope the foe won't come into our country. We are so well protected. We often see airplanes over the Redenberg, but they are not enemy ones. When the great victory came, we had no lessons. Flags were hanging everywhere. Even now the flags are still flying. Zaborze has taken your name. Good-bye, and go on hitting as hard as you can.

DEAR HERR HINDENBURG:

You are already very old and still catch so many Russians. I am very much pleased when Russians are taken prisoner. I pray every day that we may not lose. If God keeps on giving us such big victories, we certainly shan't lose. When 40,000 Russians were captured, we had a holiday. Please capture some more Russians as quickly as possible, and don't let yourself be shot dead by stupid Russians. My very best wishes.

And another young lady with ambition wrote:

I should be pleased if you would send me a little Russian. What does it look like on the battlefield? Have you been wounded

[1] In Upper Silesia.

yet? I have heard that you are very able. Has Russia still many soldiers? I hope there will soon be peace. Please write soon!

Christmas, 1914, gave astonishing proof of the esteem and affection with which Hindenburg was regarded by the German people. Over seven hundred letters arrived in which people asked whether he would find the latest remedy for rheumatism useful. Over three hundred more wished to send him means for subduing the activities of certain insects, while a further six hundred offered him tobacco, pipes, and wine. Thousands of other Christmas presents were pressed upon him. Old ladies wished to send him goloshes, and certain young ones offered pillows stuffed with their own hair!

The little sister of a war artist, for whom Hindenburg had often sat, asked him to beat the Russians again so that more school holidays would be given. In reply Hindenburg sent his best wishes to the little girl and an explanation that the Russians were being left in peace for the present only because at Christmas time there were holidays anyhow!

CHAPTER VII

THE battle of the Masurian Lakes had not quite reached its conclusion when, on September 13, the leaders of the 8th Army received a telegram from the High Command.

Withdraw two army corps as soon as possible and prepare them for transport to Krakow.

Hindenburg and his staff were puzzled. After some discussion they despatched the following telegram:

Pursuit ends tomorrow. Victory seems complete. Offensive against Narew positions possible in about ten days in settled direction. But Austria requests support by sending the army to Krakow and Upper Silesia. Four army corps and one cavalry division can be spared for this. Railway transport alone will take twenty days. Long marches towards Austrian left wing. Help reaches there late. Please send decision. Army would have, in any circumstances, to keep its independence there.

The reply of the High Command came on the next day. It read:—

Operations across the Narew considered inopportune in view of present situation of the Austrians. Direct support of the Austrians is politically essential.
Operations from Silesia come into question . . .
Independence of the army will be preserved even if co-operating with the Austrians.

Hindenburg was definitely a man who lived and moved and had his being in things military. He recognized all military expedients; he understood perfectly all military crises and knew how to deal with the means at his disposal to the greatest advantage. But political necessity? He knew nothing of that, and he hated to have politics interfere with the military. Austria's situation, her defeat by an overwhelming enemy force, had rendered immediate support a "political necessity," and on September 15, Hindenburg was obliged to part with Ludendorff, his indispensable colleague, who was appointed chief of the 9th Army which was to be reorganized in Upper Silesia. This separation, however, was only temporary, for the Kaiser's order that Hindenburg was to take over the command of the 9th Army reached him on September 17. At the same time, however, he was to hold himself at the disposal of what remained of the 8th Army in East Prussia. This force, denuded of four army corps and one cavalry division, was placed under the command of General von Schubert.

On the 18th of September in the early hours of the morning, Hindenburg left his quarters at Insterburg, by motor car, for Breslau. It was a two-day journey and he passed through his native town of Posen. The first part of the way led across the ground which had lately been the scene of such tremendous battles. He drove past ruined barns, shot-torn trees and burnt homesteads. Little by little the scene became less desolate, and districts which had been undisturbed by the War were reached. Here, however, were still pathetic sights to remind the general of what had passed. On the roads, with their faces turned eastwards again, refugees were streaming back to their home villages. They would build up their ruins again and recultivate their rav-

aged country. Many of them had lost everything in the
general chaos, but no sooner were the Russians out of the
country than they quietly returned to build up their broken
villages. Hindenburg must have felt that they were a people
worth fighting for, with their uncomplaining courage and
indestructible hope. In his thoughts he accompanied them
back along the road he had recently traveled, to their charred
and shot-riddled homes. His car bore him onwards through
simple villages and towns, where the inhabitants went peacefully about their daily work.

Hindenburg regarded the future sadly. He realized that
he was giving up his absolute independence. The telegram
from the High Command had assured him that the army
would remain independent, but his experience told him that
war fought at the side of an ally would not offer him the
same freedom of action that had been his in East Prussia.
It was not for nothing that he had studied military history
so closely. "Up to the present," he writes, "we had had our
measure of golden military freedom. But I guessed what the
future would be from the history of other coalition wars."

The troops, consisting of the 11th, 17th and 20th Reserve
Corps of Guards, a corps of militia, 35th Reserve Division,
a militia division and the 8th Cavalry Division, were brought
to the north of Krakow in close communication with the
Austro-Hungarian left wing. Headquarters were set up temporarily at Beuthen in Upper Silesia. At the end of September the centre part of the Army was marched towards Kielce.
The High Command of the Austro-Hungarian army sent a
very small army (four infantry divisions and one cavalry
division) from Krakow across the Vistula, in a northerly

direction. Hindenburg gives much credit, at this point, to the Austrian command. "They did not think they could spare more troops from the south of the river. They intended a decisive attack at this spot. This plan of our ally was bold and its originator deserved all honor. The only question was—could the greatly weakened army carry it through in spite of the support afforded them? My mind was eased to some extent by the hope that the Russians, as soon as they became aware of our German troops in Poland, would throw their full strength against us and thus make possible a success for our ally."

Meanwhile, Hindenburg and his staff had no very clear view of Russian activities. The retreating Austrians had not been pursued with any great show of determination. There were signs that a strong force of cavalry and some other troops was in readiness to the north of the Vistula. It seemed that another Russian army was being collected at Ivangorod. There was also a report that to the west of Warsaw a strong position had been taken up along a front facing west. The operations went forward and it was anticipated that, in view of the uncertain conditions, the march might at any moment undergo unexpected modifications.

Russian Poland was reached, and the men of the German armies promptly made the acquaintance of what they describe as *"Polnische Wirtschaft."* [1] "Dirt," writes Hindenburg, "was there in every form, not only in the realm of nature, but also in the so-called human habitations, and on the people themselves. In crossing our frontier, we seemed to pass into another world." There was nothing but dirt and indif-

[1] Polish husbandry.

ference everywhere; the population simply stared with dull eyes at the armies. Hindenburg was horrified by what he saw of the condition in which these degraded people lived; it seemed to him scarcely credible that such a condition should exist in the civilized world.

This time the German advance was rendered as difficult as possible by the enemy, and twelve Russian army corps were withdrawn from the main Austrian battle-front with the intention of using them against the Germans over the Vistula to the south of Ivangorod. On the 6th of October, the Germans reached the Vistula, and succeeded in repulsing the Russian troops to the west of the river. The north wing, however, was threatened from the direction of Ivangorod and Warsaw. It was therefore necessary to free this part of the line from danger before operations could be carried out in an easterly direction across the Vistula. Accordingly the German forces were marched rapidly northwards, and, on the other bank of the Vistula, the Russians moved in the same direction, towards Warsaw. To cut off the Germans, strong Russian detachments were ordered to cross the Vistula at Ivangorod and south of that town. Severe fighting took place and the Russians were beaten back, although the Germans were not able to dislodge them entirely from positions taken up on the west bank of the river. Within twenty-four hours' march of Warsaw, the German left wing under Mackensen met the enemy and forced them, though far superior in numbers, to retire. Twelve hours later, the attacking Germans were checked, but not forced to retire.

For the second time in the history of the campaign against Russia, an important document fell into the hands of the

Germans on the battlefield. This time the paper revealed the strength of the enemy, and also his intentions. There were no fewer than four Russian armies opposing the Germans—sixty divisions against eighteen. In Warsaw there were fourteen enemy divisions against five German divisions. In the scale against Germany, too, were the facts that her armies had marched over two hundred miles in fourteen days, and that the original fighting strength had been reduced, in many cases, to half and even a quarter of what they had been by the fighting in East Prussia. Hindenburg may have found himself agreeing with Henry V, who said before Agincourt that "the fewer men, the greater share of honor." Moreover, if Hindenburg, again like that warlike monarch, "coveted honor," perhaps even the immense number of troops massed against him did not daunt his spirit. He was too much of a martinet to allow himself to show any outward dismay; but inwardly he may have thought there was little chance to do anything but achieve an empty honor for his arms.

The intention of the enemy was to hold the Germans along the west bank of the Vistula, while a decisive blow should be delivered from Warsaw. This plan impressed Hindenburg greatly. The idea had emanated from the Grand Duke Nicholas; Hindenburg considered it to be the best that this general ever evolved. In 1897, he had had a short conversation with the Grand Duke on the subject of the best use of artillery. In East Prussia, Nicholas had apparently played the part of onlooker for a short period. Now Hindenburg was brought in contact with him as active opponent.

Faced with this bitter danger for, should Nicholas's plan be successful, the whole German situation in the East would be irretrievably lost—Hindenburg set himself to find means to counteract it. Again he devised a bold and simple strategical plan. It was decided to release as many troops as could possibly be spared from the Vistula line from Ivangorod southwards and concentrate them on the left wing. An attack was then to be made on Warsaw before further Russian troops could be brought there; this would deal a deathblow to the Russian plans, but its success would depend on the speed with which it could be carried out and the number of men who could be spared. The Austrian High Command was therefore requested at once to direct against Warsaw all the available divisions to the left of the Vistula. But alas! Hindenburg's forebodings as to the difficulties connected with coalition warfare were now justified. The Austrian leaders did not sufficiently realize the situation and were disposed to quibble over questions of secondary importance. Austria was prepared to support Hindenburg, but only by sending men to release the German troops from their positions on the Vistula. This, when time meant everything! Hindenburg saw one advantage: it would keep the soldiers of the two nations apart. And, as the ally to whose help he had hurried held firm, he was obliged to agree to the suggestion made, although he knew that the delay might cost him the battle.

He had reason for his anxiety. More and more Russian troops poured out of Warsaw, and some crossed the Vistula lower down. The left flank of the Germans was also in danger of being turned by the quickly developing forces spreading towards the west. In Galicia the hoped-for success had not been attained, although there it was obvious that great numbers had been withdrawn from the Austrian front and set against the German 9th Army.

The situation had to be saved. On the night of October 18, therefore, and on the 19th, the field round Warsaw was left in possession of the Russians. Mackensen's army was withdrawn to a position between Rawa and Lowicz. Hindenburg hoped that the enemy would push against this front, when he would send the corps released by the Austrians to deliver a decisive blow from the south against the strongest part of the Russian Army. But, as Hindenburg writes: "The conditions essential to the carrying out of this plan were that Mackensen's troops should be able to hold out against the attack of the Russian hordes, and that the Austro-Hungarian defence of the Vistula should stand so firmly that our intended blow would be protected against a Russian outflanking movement from the east."

The Austrian leaders had plans of their own, and they determined to allow the Russians to cross the Vistula to the north of Ivangorod and to destroy them as they came. The strategy, as Hindenburg admits, was good in itself and had often proved useful in the past. But, in view of the uncertain situation in which Germany and Austria were placed, it was fraught with grave danger. Hindenburg and his staff advised against its being attempted—but in vain. The Russians were allowed to cross, but the soldiers who had to oppose them were no Prussians. Their first success was not maintained, and presently the Austrians were in actual retreat. Hindenburg, now faced with the fact that the right wing of his attacking force was exposed, was obliged to abandon his attempt on Warsaw. It seemed best to retire for the present and to strike later in another place.

Many considerations disturbed Hindenburg. What would the people at home think as the retreat approached the German frontier? The horrors which had accompanied the occupation of East Prussia by the Russians were remembered and discussed in Silesia. Was it possible that this rich district with its flourishing mines was to suffer in a similar way?

Hindenburg's decision, however, was made, and a general retreat in the direction of Czestochowa was begun on October 27. But the retreat had to be covered somehow, and a destruction of roads and railway lines was ordered until it was found possible to work out a new plan.

Members of the staff in command were made nervous by the seemingly fatal numerical superiority of the Russians, but Hindenburg had the most complete faith in his subordinate officers and his men. At this point, however, it seemed to many that the final ruin of the German forces was only a matter of time. The Russians would choose their moment to strike. In the meantime, they celebrated their rather hollow triumph. The Germans had retired, and were apparently beaten.

But Hindenburg, thanks to his amazing attention to details, had been struck by the extraordinary use that the Russians made of Marconi messages. These were easily picked up by the Germans, who were thus in possession of a continuous supply of valuable information. On November 1, the following Marconi message was picked up by the Germans:

As we have now been in pursuit for 120 versts, we think it time to leave the following-up in the hands of the cavalry. The infantry is tired, and the going difficult.

Hindenburg and his staff, as he says, were able to draw breath and to consider their new plans. On this same day arrived a message from the Kaiser, which appointed Hindenburg Commander-in-Chief of all the German armies in the East. Ludendorff remained his chief of staff. The leadership of the 9th Army was given to General von Mackensen. Hindenburg decided to make his headquarters at Posen, but, on November 3, before leaving Czestochowa, he completed the plans for the next part of the campaign. There could be no question of launching an attack against the heavily defended front line, for that would simply mean disaster. It must be aimed, instead, at the poorly protected flank. The position of the north wing of the enemy, in the neighborhood of Lodz, was considered, and it was seen that the German attacking army would have to be brought as far as Thorn. The new movement was directed toward positions betwen Thorn and Gnesen, which meant a very wide separation from the Austro-Hungarian left wing. To make possible the carrying out of the German advance, Austria's leaders would have to withdraw four infantry divisions from the Carpathian front to take the place of the troops withdrawn from Czestochowa to the south.

This northward march divided the Eastern armies into three groups. The first was composed of the Austro-Hungarian soldiers on both banks of the upper reaches of the Vistula; the second and third were, respectively, the 8th and 9th German Armies. It was impossible to fill the gaps.

The area of over sixty miles which stretched between the Austrians and the 9th Army was filled by inexperienced troops. They were pathetically few in number as compared with their opponents, and were so widely spread out that they could scarcely be described as a fighting line. Hindenburg knew that by sheer force of numbers the Russians could force their way into Silesia at any time. Between the 9th Army at Thorn and the 8th Army in East Prussia there was also a very small muster of troops—a few front-line men and a few reserves—against which four army corps of Russians were held in readiness to the north of Warsaw. It was conceivable that these troops might be moved forward so as to reproduce the situation that had preceded the battle of Tannenberg.

The 9th Army had therefore to beat the Russians on their flank, and it was plain that the blow must fall swiftly and surely, or this comparatively small force would be annihilated by the chief strength of the Russian army in a concentrated attack. The 8th Army, in spite of its precarious position, was obliged to send two army corps to the 9th Army. Two cavalry divisions were brought from the western front, and the attacking force was thus composed of five and a half army corps and five cavalry divisions. It was set in movement on November 11—not a moment too soon, for an enemy Marconi message revealed the fact that an attack, intended to penetrate into Germany, had been planned along the whole of the northwest front. This was to have taken place on November 14, but on the 13th the Russians became aware of the German attack and did not venture to carry out the intended blow against Silesia. Thus one of the main hopes of Hindenburg—the saving of Silesia—was for the moment fulfilled. Meanwhile the 9th Army was engaged in the fiercest conflict which had yet been waged on the eastern front. Every inch of ground was savagely contested. The enemy numbers seemed to preclude all chance of a decisive victory, but Hindenburg still hoped for one. Alternately attacking and defending, surrounding and being surrounded, the Prussian army exerted its utmost strength. The Russians could not advance and it became clear that, for the time being, little was to be feared. The question arose—could Germany and Austria not only hold in check the hordes against them, but indeed compel them to return whence they had come? Reinforcements were sent from the western front, but these troops, though brave and willing, were worn out. They had just come from the battle of Ypres, and this struggle, together with their long journey eastward, had exhausted them. Hindenburg determined to attempt to force the Russian army to retreat, but, as the reinforcements reached him only piecemeal and the troops opposing him were so numerous, he could do nothing decisive. The Russians withdrew a short distance and lay still, worn out by the long fighting.

Then Nature and the elements laid a paralyzing grip on friend and foe alike—winter covered the countryside with frost and snow and to some extent silenced the guns. Russians and Germans lay in their encampments, and waited through the long, weary months. What would happen when the spring returned? At any rate, the German soldiers could rest satisfied that they had done their duty and had indeed proved themselves worthy of the trust which their leader had placed in them.

CHAPTER VIII

THE winter passed silently, except for certain small and localized activities. And it was Hindenburg's armies that started the battle again. In the Carpathians, however, the Germans and Austrians had a terrible struggle to keep the Hungarian country safe. Ludendorff had been obliged to pay a visit to this part of the line; he returned with very serious news of the conditions there, and feeling no little anxiety about the Austro-Slav divisions of the army. The need for decisive victory for Austria was not only a military but a political one. There was already unrest in the country and fear that the war might not end well. Moreover, the attitude of Italy was such that the Austrians felt insecure; their troops were menaced from the rear. A great victory in the east was, therefore, a matter of daily increasing urgency.

At the beginning of 1915, four army corps, some from France and some from home, were placed at Hindenburg's disposal. These men were brought through the bitter weather in trains which, for the most part, were unheated. They disentrained in East Prussia. Some were sent to increase the strength of the 8th Army, and some were added to the 10th under General von Eichhorn. Extra support was sent to both wings of the German front line from Lötzen to Gumbinnen. In the headquarters at Posen, the plan of action was prepared and discussed, and it was determined that the 10th Russian Army should be surrounded, that the two German flanking movements should meet on Russian ground, and that as much as possible of the Russian fighting force should be destroyed.

On the 5th of February, from Insterburg, where Hindenburg and his staff had moved to conduct the offensive, orders to attack were issued. On the 7th both wings started to move and the circle widened and then swept closely round the enemy troops. Winter still held the land in its icy grip; the marching men had to suffer no little privation in the bitter cold. But they moved relentlessly onward, and on February 21 the circle was completed. Hindenburg had once again lived up to his own phrase: "Boldness coupled with caution." His manœuvre was completely successful. From this battleground he was able to see once more the long, tattered columns of Russian prisoners passing to captivity. They numbered over one hundred thousand. Many more lay dead upon the frozen fields. However, it was impossible for Hindenburg to follow up this blow immediately; for, to replace the lost men, thousands of fresh troops were brought up, released from parts of the line where they were not needed. The numbers of Russians were too great to permit an attempt to be made to annihilate another part of their army. Savage battles were fought, which ended mostly on Russian ground. War raged starkly in the Carpathians where the Russians endeavored, even through the winter, to force their way over the Hungarian frontier. It seemed to the Russians that success in this undertaking would bring a decisive moment in the whole war; that Austria could never survive so awful a blow. The situation was grave in the extreme, but the German High Command found a way out of the danger. At the beginning of May the Russian force in north Galicia was broken through and the enemy front on the Hungarian frontier was successfully attacked on the flank and in the rear. Hindenburg's share in this work was indirect. He was instructed to engage the enemy forces which might otherwise have been released and sent to the Carpathian front. Accordingly, he attacked the Russians to the west of Warsaw and at the East Prussian frontier. On April 27 a cavalry force was sent into Kurland and Lithuania. Three cavalry divisions supported by infantry threatened the chief railway lines which were the principal communications of the Russian army. To prevent disaster, the enemy sent strong forces to this part of the line, but the contest in Lithuania continued until the summer. More German troops were sent thither to hold the occupied territory; and thus little by little the Niemen Army was created.

Gradually the front extended and blazed into action. The southern part of the Russian front was pressed back. The northern pressed a strong flank between the Vistula and the swamp district. The plans for another great attack began to take shape. Should this new attack, which would press forward from East Prussia, pass to the east or the west of the Bobr swamp district? The High Command decided that the westerly direction was the better. The attack was ordered to pass across the lower reaches of the Narew. The army under Gallwitz swept down upon the Narew, and Hindenburg went personally into the battlefield. He remained with the army for two days and witnessed the capture of the town Przasnysz. On the 17th of July, Gallwitz's army reached the Narew. Once again faced with the possibility of being encircled, the Russians began, little by little, to withdraw along the whole line of battle. But, as Hindenburg says, the fruits of victory could not be gathered in a pursuit of the retiring hordes, but would be reaped in full measure if an attack were pressed towards Vilna, to force the Russian centre back upon the swamps and to cut off their lines of communication. The High Command, however, ordered pursuit. At this time, the fortress of Nowo Georgiewsk fell into the hands of the Germans, a matter of strategic importance because the railway between Mlawa and Warsaw passed through it. On the 18th of August Hindenburg met the Kaiser and rode in his train through the recently captured town. It presented a dreary spectacle, for the Russians had carried out a very wholesale destruction before they had made surrender. The barracks were still in flames. Large groups of prisoners were being shepherded together. Everything that could have proved of use to the Germans had been destroyed; all the horses had been shot. Hindenburg testifies to the astonishing thoroughness with which the Russians destroyed what they could no longer hold.

In July the German Niemen Army was moved eastwards. In the middle of August, Kovno was captured by the 10th Army. But there were never a sufficient number of troops to enable the German leader to carry out his ideas. It was possible only to pursue and embarrass the retreating Russians. On the 9th of September a move was made upon Vilna, the way having been cleared by the Niemen Army in July. Hindenburg was filled with apprehension. Perhaps this undertaking would be crowned with another enormous success; perhaps there would be more long green-grey lines of prisoners—but perhaps the move had been made too late. Over Vilna to the south came the German army; but the Russians were aware of the danger that threatened their communications. The battles round Vilna were waged with the fury of men who saw themselves trapped. Every passing moment meant one more degree of safety for the Russians. The German cavalry divisions which had hoped to lay hands upon the railway were beaten back. This time the plan failed. The blow had been struck too late, and the magnificent fighting spirit of the German troops had not availed to save the day.

In October, 1915, Hindenburg removed his headquarters to Kovno. The winter of 1915-1916 was much quieter, and Hindenburg was able to hunt now and then and to enjoy sleighing runs through the whitened countryside. In many divisions the soldiers employed their leisure in editing trench newspapers, and some of these published stories about their Commander-in-Chief. One such story refers to Hindenburg's well-known objection to traffic blocks. This was the occasion of constant anxiety to divisional chiefs. If Hindenburg's car happened to appear upon the scene and were held up for any reason, there was always trouble for someone. The commandant of a frontier town was therefore not a little distressed when he saw a solid mass of sheep trotting along a road for which he was responsible. He was hoping to be able to drive the animals away, and praying that the great man might not pass down that road, when the horn of Hindenburg's car was heard. But on this occasion the general was in excellent humor. Catching sight of the trembling commandant, he observed pleasantly: "Well, Colonel! I have just seen your picked troops going down the road!" The unfortunate man started to make some excuse, when Hindenburg spoke again. "Don't worry," he remarked kindly. "They were in excellent marching order!" And the car rolled on, while the commandant sighed his relief.

Once during the winter, Hindenburg went to the woods of Augustow to shoot wolves, but, as he relates, the wolves kept away and the expedition proved vain. There were by this time few traces left of the ghastly struggles that had taken place in the past summer and autumn. Trenches still stood, but for the most part the battlegrounds had been cleared.

Although the winter was quieter so far as actual fighting was concerned, Ludendorff and Hindenburg had the colossal task on their shoulders of supplying the armies with food, winter clothing, and other necessities, and preserving good feeling between the soldiers and the civil population. Ludendorff identified himself very closely with all this organization work, and was given an absolutely free hand by Hindenburg, who never interfered with any colleague or subordinate who carried out his work with competence and good faith.

At Kovno, in April, 1916, Hindenburg completed the fiftieth year of his military service. This was the occasion of a little celebration, but, as the fighting had broken out again in March, Hindenburg had little time to give to personal matters. Anxiety lay heavily upon him, for not only did he have to think about the military situation, but he had

to ensure that his troops were preserved from the twin enemies, hunger and disease. Though the winter of 1915-16
was considerably quieter, yet hostilities kept breaking out
at various parts of the line, and it was quite impossible to
connect these with any definite plan. Hindenburg considered the districts round Smorgon Dunaburg and Riga as
danger-points for the Germans, because the chief Russian
railways passed through them. Just in these parts, however,
no signs of Russian activity were manifested.

On March 18, the Russian attack was launched, precisely
where it was not expected, at Lake Narocz and at Postawy.
One hundred and twenty-eight Russian battalions were hurled
against nineteen German battalions. A most intense barrage
upon the German positions prepared the way for the attack.
The conditions in the German trenches were appalling. The
few troops were standing, in some places, breast-high in icy
water. Thaw had set in and the field was nothing but a
swamp. The breastwork of the trenches started to wash
away, rendering the discomfort of the men more acute than
ever. They withstood the barrage, and they withstood the
murderous onslaughts of the Russian hosts by returning a
ceaseless fire. Wave after wave of enemy soldiers replaced
those slain; the dead lay in heaps before the German lines.
And still the few held fast, refused to be driven back. The
attack wavered at last and broke. The Russians were beaten
once more, and the few heroic troops stood victors, this time
on the shores of Narocz Lake. The Russian losses were esti-
mated at 140,000.

And now news from the western battle front began to
monopolize attention. Would the German armies there suc-

ceed in capturing Verdun? The word "Italy," too, was heard on many lips, and a plan for an Austro-Hungarian attack upon that country was discussed, together with its chances of success. The plan was a bold one—but how was it to be carried out? If the flower of the Austro-Hungarian Army were to attack Italy, what would be the result upon the eastern frontier? How, then, would the Russians be held in check? Reports of victories came from the Italian front, but Hindenburg viewed the situation with doubt and distress, and, before long, his fears were justified.

On June 4, the Austro-Hungarian troops gave before the Russian attack in the districts of Volhynia and in Bukowina. "This time," writes Hindenburg, "there was no victorious German army at hand to save the situation; in the west the battle raged round Verdun, and signs of storm were threatening from the Somme."

Fortune was in one respect favorable. The Russians did not renew their attack on the German troops; they were hurried to the help of their allies, as many as could be spared. One part of the Austrian front, consisting of German, Austrian and Hungarian troops, held fast under the leadership of General Graf Bothmer. The Germans from East Prussia were entrained and carried south to the battlefields of Galicia. And, at this time, bad news of a threatened breakdown of the German army in France came through to depress the leaders in the east. Hindenburg and Ludendorff were twice called to Pless to consult with the Kaiser at his headquarters. The Austrians had been forced to accede to a condition in return for the help accorded to them from East Prussia. Hindenburg's command, by this condition, was extended east of Lemberg, and strong Austro-Hungarian forces were made subject to his orders. Hindenburg visited his new command at the earliest possible moment, and found there "a willingness to meet him and an unreserved criticism of their own weakness." A strong hand was needed to deal with the army of mixed nationalities, and Hindenburg moved his headquarters to Brest-Litovsk. There, on August 28, he received an urgent summons from the Kaiser to come immediately to General Headquarters. "The situation was serious." In addition to all the troubles with which Germany was beset, there was now another: Roumania had made her declaration of war.

On August 29, Hindenburg reached Pless, in company with his chief of staff. He expected that he would be called upon to express his views and to discuss plans with the Kaiser. What actually happened was that he was now appointed Chief of the General Staff of the German Armies, while Ludendorff was made 1st Quartermaster-General. In the space of two years, the former infantry general was promoted first to the command of the army and then to the chieftainship of the fighting forces of the whole nation. His predecessor, General von Falkenhayn, gave him his hand in farewell. "God help you and our Fatherland," he said.

The situation was, indeed, serious. Verdun had not been taken, and the battle of the Somme had not redounded to Germany's advantage. German hopes had not entirely faded, but they were dim. In the southern part of the Carpathians the Russians were pushing forward, and it was a matter of doubt whether the Hungarian boundary line could be held. Owing to the failure of their armies in Galicia, the

Austro-Hungarian attack in South Tyrol had to be abandoned, and the Italians were advancing, though the outnumbered defending troops exhibited the greatest heroism. Bulgaria was in difficulties and Roumania had entered the war. Everywhere the enemy forces seemed to have the upper hand, and the German and Austro-Hungarian reserves were very few. The unfavorable military situation was made worse by the bad conditions at home. That most terrible enemy of all—hunger—stalked amid the ranks of the non-combatants, who besides were disheartened at the news from all of the fronts. Men, women and children were faced with starvation, and, although Hindenburg writes that there was as yet no reason to suppose the population would not hold out, still there was cause for anxiety. The patience of hungry people is notoriously small. Not only in Germany but also in Austria the food shortage was beginning to be seriously felt. Political and domestic affairs are not, except indirectly, the business of a commander-in-chief, but such was the general situation at the time when Hindenburg took over the highest post which the army had to offer, and it is certain that the knowledge of the bad conditions at home played its part in his mind.

It was obvious that there must be a union between the leaders of the armies on the different fronts, and so Hindenburg, acting for the *Oberste Kriegsleitung,* was given the power to make agreements with the leaders of the German allies.

Pless, a small town in Upper Silesia, had been decided upon as a suitable spot for general headquarters, because it was near the town of Teschen, where the Austrian headquarters had been set up. During the time which Hindenburg spent at Pless, he met most of the chief political and military personalities of Germany and her allies. King Ferdinand of Bulgaria was one of those who most deeply impressed the field marshal, who regarded the king's political and diplomatic qualities as brilliant. "His political vision," writes Hindenburg of this monarch, "extended far beyond the boundaries of the Balkans. He perfectly understood how to use the great political conflicts of the world to the advantage of his own country, so as to push it into the foreground."

On the eve of November, 1916, the Emperor of Austria died, and his death was an irreparable blow not only to his own country but to Germany. The young Emperor Charles was not the man to wrestle with a situation which was already nearly hopeless. He removed Conrad from the command of the Austrian armies on the eastern frontier and put in his place General von Arz, a man of only moderate abilities. Conrad's successes had been few and inconspicuous, but this was due rather to ill fortune than to anything else. His star had not been a lucky one, but his performance under the worst possible conditions had been more than creditable. His successor was inactive and without any considerable powers of leadership, and he was certainly no substitute for the tireless and able Conrad. Well might Hindenburg say: "With the honored, grey-haired Emperor, a large part of the national conscience of this country of many races sank almost into the grave." The efforts of the Emperor Charles to reconcile the different sections of his people failed completely.

At Pless, too, in 1916, Hindenburg met Enver Pasha, the

military leader of Turkey, and General Jekoff of Bulgaria. Enver Pasha impressed Hindenburg as a man of clear insight and decision. When asked by the German leader for a description of the situation in Turkey, he replied with an amazing clarity and certainty. "The position of Turkey in Asia," he said, "is to some extent very difficult. We must fear a possibility that we shall be thrown further back in Armenia. It is also not impossible that the fighting in Iraq will soon break out again. Also, I believe that the English will soon be in a position to attack us through Syria with larger forces than we have. But whatever may happen in Asia, the outcome of the war will be decided upon European ground, and for this I place all my available divisions at your disposal."

General Jekoff of Bulgaria, however, was another type of man. He was, writes Hindenburg, "not without sober powers of observation and was capable of great thoughts," but it is also plain that he was a soldier first, a soldier second, and a soldier third. That is to say, he had limitations. His men had an extravagant admiration for him, and his trust in their fighting ability was almost fantastic. Once, someone suggested that these soldiers might hesitate to confront the Russians, and his emphatic reply was: "If I tell my Bulgarians they are to fight, they will do so—let it be against whom it may!"

Hindenburg met at Pless not only the military chiefs of the German allies, but also their political leaders. Talaat Pasha semes to have impressed him very deeply as a man of great gifts. He was fully aware of the enormous difficulties of his position, but, as Hindenburg says, no statesman can supply in a few months what has been neglected for centuries. The country had no national feeling, and though the victories at the Dardanelles served to give it some little national pride for a time, the spell of the black centuries of the past still prevailed.

Such were the leading personalities of the countries allied with Germany, and with these Hindenburg was empowered to discuss means and measures and carry them out.

CHAPTER IX

On August 27 Roumania declared war on Austria, and on August 28 on Germany, and five armies took the field. Mackensen's army started operations against Roumania on September 5, and completely routed its opponents.

The 9th German Army was also brought to Roumania, but it was badly delayed by the Hungarians, who offered passive resistance and whose traffic officials increased by deliberate incompetence the inefficiency of the railway service. In the middle of November this army forced its way into the mountains. Intense frost and increasing storms, the scarcity of roads and the resistance offered by a brave enemy were again contended against and overcome by the Germans. Bucharest was occupied on December 6, but it was out of the question to attempt with so few men to dislodge the enemy from his strong positions in the mountains. The Roumanian Army, with French support, undertook a useless attack upon Mackensen's army in July, 1917. A few localized actions took place but were without importance, and an armistice with Roumania was concluded in December, 1917.

The difficulties which the German leaders were called upon to face in 1916 were greatly sharpened by the action of Sarrail's army on the Macedonian front. The Bulgarians, who had exhibited the greatest valor in attack, weakened under the artillery fire to which they were then subjected.

They were driven from the positions they had won, and supports had to be hurried to their aid—supports which had been destined for Roumania. Turkey also hurried to the assistance of Bulgaria, with a whole army corps. But Hindenburg writes: "These supports were not welcomed by Bulgaria, because she feared that, as a result of accepting them, undesired Turkish claims might be made in the sphere of politics. Enver Pasha, however, assured us that he would prevent any such developments." The retreat of the Bulgarian army was not regarded as a disaster by Hindenburg, because the general situation of the Bulgarian soldiers was rather improved by retirement upon stronger positions, while that of their enemy was rendered more difficult.

Hindenburg, whose pride in the German army was almost boundless, in his memoirs compares the qualities of the Bulgarian and German soldiers.

"For the first time, the Bulgarians found themselves in positions that it was hard for them to defend. Although previous reports from our officers had always praised the magnificent spirit of Bulgarian soldiers in attack, now a certain sensitiveness was revealed in them when they had to face continuous fire from the enemy artillery. . . . It may be that modern methods of attack, with their nerve-destroying features, demand in the defence something besides inherent strength, some element produced only by a highly developed will-power. The proper combination of morale and bodily strength seems to characterize most of our German soldiery." No one who views with an unprejudiced eye the deeds of the German army during four years of war, will care to dispute the field marshal's words.

Hindenburg, as chief of the German armies, had now to turn his attention to the east. What was the position there in the year 1916? The Russian offensive in Armenia, which had been anxiously watched by Germany, came suddenly to a stop. The attempted offensive against the left wing of this Russian advance failed completely. The difficult country through which it had to make its way and the seeming hopelessness of setting up proper communications made it impossible to move forward. In addition the early descent of winter rendered it likely that Russia would try, before the cold weather set in, to reach a final decision.

The Turkish armies in the Caucasus were in a terrible condition. It was not enough that they had fought and bled and that there were many killed and wounded. Other privations were added to the usual miseries of war. They had insufficient food, procured with difficulty; and they had no proper clothing. Only barest necessities reached them, carried to their positions not by trains nor by beasts of burden, but by women and children. Hundreds of these died by the wayside, lacking the stamina for the long marches of many days' duration. In Iraq, Kut-el-Amara had been taken, but Hindenburg had no reason to think that its loss would be quietly accepted by the English, and he did not believe that the Turks were strong enough to resist the attack when it came. He advised that the forces there should be strengthened. But Turkey "for political reasons" sent an army corps to Persia instead. Well might Hindenburg deplore that political consideration had a baneful influence on military operations. In Palestine, the outlook was bleak. The Turkish troops had failed in August, 1916, in the second attack upon the Suez Canal. By degrees they had been forced back upon Gaza. The English were constructing a railway from Egypt, and it seemed that it would not be long before the Turks would again be attacked. Hindenburg wondered, not without apprehension, what effect the loss of Jerusalem would be likely to have upon his allies of the Crescent. In Syria, as in the Caucasus, the Turkish troops suffered terribly from lack of proper communication lines. Crops failed, and there was a scarcely veiled hostility to be faced on the part of the Arabs.

Many considerations tempted Hindenburg to increase the numbers of troops in Mesopotamia and Syria. In unguarded moments he dreamed great dreams of empire, such dreams as come to every military leader, but he knew them to be fantastic and put them from him. How it might be possible to push forces through Syria to Egypt, to threaten India through Persia and Afghanistan, were questions that came into his mind. They were but chimerical fancies, for, if it was not possible to feed and clothe even the small forces in Mesopotamia and Syria, what would happen to greater armies? They would perish of thirst and famine. It was impossible under these conditions to try to plan such ventures.

Meanwhile fearful battles raged round Verdun and on the Somme. Because there were insufficient German troops, Hindenburg could not organize attacks for the relief of the men engaged on these great slaughter-grounds. Soon after he took over the command of the armies, he felt compelled to recommend that the Kaiser give orders to cease attacks on Verdun. The losses which these attacks were causing

Germany were so serious that it seemed as if an artery had been cut in the body of the country; the blood was precious, the waning strength would be hard to renew. The name "Verdun" had the same sound as the word "hell" in the ears of the German soldiery. The people at home, however, waited and watched for news of the capture of Verdun —that news which would mean that the many sacrificed lives had not been laid down in vain. The nerves of the non-combatant population were strained almost to breaking-point, and Hindenburg wished to save them from the fearful reaction that would certainly follow upon the publication of unfavorable news. He hoped, too, that when German attacks ceased, the French would content themselves with purely defensive measures. In this he was mistaken, for in October they made their swift attack along the east bank of the river Meuse. The Germans were unable to withstand it, and Douaumont fell. The attack was preceded by an artillery fire which broke down what little strength remained in the German troops. In the month of December the struggle round Verdun was brought to a close—the French had triumphed.

All the world knows the history of the Somme, and how the fierce and wearying months went by, taking their toll on both sides. Hindenburg directs some criticism against the commanders of the Allied Armies, which is certainly justified. In his *Aus meinem Leben* he writes:

If our western opponents were not able to achieve a decisive victory in the campaigns of 1915-17, this must chiefly be attributed to a certain partiality on the part of their leaders. The enemy certainly did not lack the necessary numbers of men, apparatus and ammunition; and one cannot say that the opposing troops were not good enough to respond to the requirements of an active and skilful leadership. In addition, our western enemy had at his disposal well-developed railway and road communications, and also everything needful for the best possible development of a much greater freedom to operate. The opposing leaders did not make the fullest use of these. That we were able to hold out so long was certainly due, in addition of course to other considerations, to a certain unfruitfulness of the ground upon which the enemy plans ripened. In spite of this, however, the demands which were made upon our leaders and upon our men on those battlefields were monstrous.

In September, well aware that he must immediately acquaint himself with the situation on the western front, Hindenburg visited it in company with Ludendorff. On the way, they were joined by the Kaiser and the Crown Prince. Hindenburg refers constantly to the pleasantness of his relations with his monarch and to the excellence of the Kaiser's military judgments. At Cambrai, Hindenburg, at the command of the Kaiser, handed over the Prussian field marshal's bâtons to the heirs to the thrones of Bavaria and Württemberg. This ceremony was followed by a prolonged conference with the army leaders of the western front. The principal troubles were the inferior numbers of the German airplanes and artillery and the relative lack of ammunition. Hindenburg was deeply struck with what he saw of the conditions on the Somme. Here were men who had never experienced a single moment of "soldiers' good fortune," whose war horizon consisted of trenches and shell-holes, and in whose ears the sound of artillery bombardment rang incessantly. Their whole duty had been simply to stay were they were, to hold out to the very last ounce of their strength and, if necessary, beyond it. Hindenburg knew only too well the value of a successful offensive to the morale of soldiers and the daily sapping of the strength of will and body which a long, eventless defence must always occasion. He fully understood that both officers and men pined to escape from these awful conditions, but, he writes, "many of our best and most enthusiastic soldiers had to shed their heart's blood in broken trenches" before the day for the attack dawned. At last, the savage phase of the battle of the Somme abated somewhat, when the rainy season set in. The ground became like a quagmire and the shell-holes filled with water. Neither the Germans nor their enemies could talk of victory; and both sides only lay wearily under the grey skies and splashed their way about in the soaking trenches. Even now, however, there was not complete still-ness, for the guns still thundered sullenly, and the name "Somme" began to sound as evil in the soldiers' ears as the name "Verdun".

CHAPTER X

WITH his acceptance of the highest post in the army, Hindenburg was obliged to occupy himself to some extent with questions relating to politics. His skill and perspicacity in all military questions, however complicated these might be, and his patience in working out every detail with due thoroughness, were qualities which he was unable to carry into the realm of politics. And he hated diplomacy. There is evidence of asperity and of some lack of understanding in his own writings on the subject. "The ins and outs of all these countless political questions and counter-questions only brought me uncomfortable hours and increased my dislike of politics."

The first such question with which Hindenburg had to concern himself was that of Polish independence. In the resurrection of Poland, he saw some dangers to Germany. The Austrians thought to attach the Catholic districts of Poland to themselves, but, in August, 1916, the Germans and Austrians came to an agreement in Vienna, by which they decided to make Poland an independent kingdom as soon as possible. General von Falkenhayn, however, who had succeeded Hindenburg as commander of the eastern front, raised prompt objection to this agreement and the Kaiser supported him. The existence of such an agreement, however, could not be concealed for ever; it was soon a matter of common discussion. The Governor-General of Warsaw, therefore, soon after Hindenburg's acceptance of the High Command, demanded that Poland be immediately proclaimed a kingdom; he offered to introduce conscription by way of lending support to the German army. Hindenburg, in view of the pressing need for such support, was willing to use his influence to set up Poland as a kingdom, but he and those who thought like him were opposed by the government. There was some possibility of being able to come to terms with Russia, and it was feared that the Czar and his ministers would be offended if such a step were taken.

While planning out the Roumanian campaign, Hindenburg was approached with regard to a peace settlement; he met this with a strong, even passionate approval, although he had small hopes that it could be successful. He gave his full attention to the details of the peace offer, but was determined that "neither the army nor the country should suffer through it." The Kaiser, he writes, was convinced that the offer could not fail entirely, and on December 12, the allied countries were informed of Germany's willingness to make peace. The offer was rejected, and was followed by President Wilson's attempt to bring peace to the world. At last came the fatal day in February, 1917, when Germany handed to America her conditions for peace accompanied by her declaration of unlimited U-boat warfare. The result was America's declaration of war on Germany; and certain South American states followed her lead. Germany ultimately stood opposed to twenty-eight countries; three-quarters of the world was at war with her.

Home politics also pressed for attention, and Hindenburg

worked out his great war industry program. In this, as he says himself, his chief care was to ensure that the fighting forces should receive what they needed. All other considerations were subordinated to this primary one. The program was sharply criticized by post-war politicians and thinkers. Hindenburg writes: "After the war, it was said that this program had been dictated by a distracted mind. The phrase-maker who used this expression was completely in error with regard to the spirit in which the program was conceived." Hindenburg kept his head in every emergency; here and there he may have made mistakes, but such mistakes were never the result of "distraction." In his long service with the army in wartime and in peace, his instincts and his early training served to keep him true to his course. Even in the wildest tumults and storms, he never allowed himself to drift rudderless upon the sea of despair.

He now threw himself with all his ardor into putting through the *Kriegshilfsdienst* [1] law. He wished to see put at the disposal of their country, not only all men who could possibly bear arms, but all men (and also women) who were capable of work at all. At this stage of the war, he must have seen disaster coming, but he was determined that the country—if fall it must—should go down fighting to the last ditch. Every group must be employed, and every faculty exerted. Perhaps he thought that a gigantic effort might still save the situation. But here he was doomed to disappointment. "The final form of the law was a different and far more modest one than that which I had conceived. . . . The law was finally based upon political and com-

[1] War Aid Service.

mercial considerations, and failed adequately to express the deeply rooted spirit of the whole Fatherland."

The makers of this law were bitterly reproached that they had placed the country in an economic and social situation which was to no small extent responsible for the Revolution. Certain it is that, in spite of regulations fixing the maximum prices of many daily necessaries, the merchants who dealt in these goods found means to evade the rules. These necessaries were simply withdrawn from the open market and were to be obtained only by those who had the money to pay the exorbitant prices demanded. Those who could pay had plenty in their larders, but the great bulk of the middle classes suffered the bitterest need. Starvation and all the diseases that hunger brings in its train had to be faced. It was small wonder that the despairing population began to murmur threateningly. The halo which had shone around the soldiers at the beginning of the war was now sadly tarnished; the army began to lose its romantic glamor in the eyes of the dispirited people.

In addition to the pressing food trouble, there was, owing to lack of raw material, insufficient clothing in the country. The needs of the soldiers had to be met, and soon it was necessary to issue clothing coupons. Upon the wealthier classes was laid the duty of giving away what they could spare from their wardrobes; but, as may well be imagined, there were many such who did not respond readily to the demands made.

The *Kriegshilfsdienst* law gave many opportunities to the conscienceless profiteer to enrich himself. Many thousands of people lived in plenty and indifference while the soldiers hungered and died on the battle-fronts and the middle classes starved and murmured. There was soon a dangerous gap between the army and the population, which it seemed hopeless to try to bridge. Hindenburg had hoped that this law would weld the country into a great home army, working —as vigorously as the men at the fronts were fighting—for the common weal of the Fatherland. But the form that it took finally was not the form in which he had conceived it.

The Kaiser and the government were too much occupied with the soldiers to see the fearful precipice towards which the domestic régime was headed. They forgot that wars are not won solely in the field, and they did not fully realize the need for a strong, properly organized home policy. The reins of state lay idle in their hands, and they placed all their hopes upon the army and upon the result which an unlimited U-boat warfare was likely to have upon England. Some result it certainly had, for food there had to be rationed, but no real need arose such as was experienced in Germany. Even a hungry population if tactfully and strongly led, might not have fallen into revolution.

The year 1917 dawned, and Hindenburg knew what he had to expect from the Allies' armies. An attack would certainly be made all along the line, and it was essential that the powers of resistance of the German army should be increased to the maximum. To Hindenburg it did not seem likely that the mistakes made by the Allied leaders in 1916 would be repeated, and he longed to be able to surprise them before their attack could be launched. He had neither the troops nor the materials which such a surprise required. The end of 1916 had found Germany in a well-nigh hopeless condition. In the summer of 1916, the Serbian army had reappeared on the scene of war, and it must be mentioned that its ranks were increased by many Slav deserters from the Austro-Hungarian Army.

Many people speak of the "fortunes of war" and of "the chances of war," but to Hindenburg such phrases seemed as idle and empty as the wind. Chance, he considered, plays a negligible part. "Long after the war," he wrote, "I saw in the war's course and outcome, even when the latter went against us, an inexorable logical sequence. Whoever attacks, and is in a position to attack, has success on his side; whoever omits, or is obliged to omit, an attack, loses."

Threatening though the position on the western front was for Germany, Hindenburg was obliged to admit to himself that an even greater danger was to be feared in the east from the hordes of Russia. The morale in the Austro-Hungarian army was such that he dared not remove the German support which had been accorded to this ally; and it seemed likely that this would even have to be increased. German officers in Macedonia were using their influence and their experience gained on other battle-fronts to spread the right spirit throughout the Bulgarian army, but Hindenburg had to reckon with the probable need of having to send supports also to this country.

On the Somme, Hindenburg felt that the situation might be saved by an attack, and he considered ways and means; again he had to come to the conclusion that an attack at this part of the line would be too great a risk. After the months of bitter fighting that had occurred here, the German line along a length of about thirty miles had been forced to yield up a depth of about six miles of country. This Allied success had been accompanied by appalling losses on both sides, and Germany was recruiting her losses from an underfed population. Hindenburg decided against attack and in favor of retreat, and the men were therefore withdrawn to the line through Arras, St. Quentin and Soissons. The withdrawal started on March 16, 1917, and the Allied troops pursued cautiously over the once fair countryside. The position now taken up was known as the Siegfried Line, and the shortened front line improved the conditions under which the German army fought. Strong reserves were brought up, and Hindenburg considered the question of attacking the Allies with some of these fresh troops; and he felt safer as he realized that he had now so disposed his soldiers that he could attack weak spots in the opposing line at any moment.

The decision to retire upon the "Siegfried Line" had been reached only after long and anxious discussion. Its probable effect upon the men who had fought so desperately to hold the ground now yielded up was likely to be depressing—its effect upon the civil population which had waited so long and vainly for tidings of victory was likely to be even dangerous; but Hindenburg risked giving the upper hand to the enemy for the moment, in order to improve conditions for the army.

General von Conrad had suggested at the end of 1916 that a great attack should be made upon Italy, where he believed that, with some help from Germany, there was a good chance of decisive victory and an advantageous peace with at least one of the opposing powers. He stressed the good effect that such a victory would have on the spirit of the Austrian soldiers. Hindenburg, however, refused his consent to such a scheme. He pointed out that even defeat would probably not force Italy into making peace, and that her complete overthrow would never be tolerated by the Allied armies. England, especially, would hasten to help her, and German supports were needed for other and more urgent work. Bulgaria, too, was eager to attack the Allies in Macedonia, where she saw possibilities of forcing the enemy to evacuate that country, and she directed a hungry gaze upon Salonika. But Hindenburg had objections here, too. "Had we forced the Entente troops to evacuate Macedonia," he writes, "we should have had them hurled upon us at the western front." And the Bulgarians "quite rightly" did not feel able to carry out any successful attack without the support of at least six German divisions, which Hindenburg was not prepared to send to their aid.

Turkey was in a bad way. All that Germany could ask her to do was to defend herself and engage the forces that stood over against her that they might not also be added to the numbers against which Germany was contending. In August, 1916, she was warned to withdraw her ill-fed armies from the Armenian mountains so that they need not suffer the privations of winter; but the necessary orders were given too late. These Turkish forces were almost entirely disintegrated by the sufferings they had undergone. Intense cold descended upon them and they had not even enough clothing. The food columns, themselves unable to cope with the dreadful conditions, were not regular with their scanty supplies. The Turks died by hundreds, not upon the field

of honor and not contending with a foe against whom they
had some chance, but of starvation and of inexorable cold.
And there was none to help them in that wild, depopulated
district. "No song," writes Hindenburg, "no roll of honor,
will ever relate their tragic end."

In March, 1917, came an event which at that moment was
not looked for. The Russian Revolution broke out, and it
seemed that here was the opportunity for a German offensive
against her eastern enemy. The news was received with
dismay by the Allies, and the greatest possible influence was
brought to bear upon the new leaders to compel them to
hold the German troops upon the eastern front. Somehow
this had to be achieved until American soldiers could be
brought to France.

Germany hoped for rest but was at first disappointed.
Kerensky held his front, and there were attacks against the
whole line. In the north Germany held out, but the Austro-
Hungarian troops were able to stand against the enemy only
in those positions where they received German help. At
Stanislau, indeed, the Russians broke through, but they did
not follow up their victory. Meanwhile powerful influences
were at work behind the Russian armies. Many men deserted
because they were anxious about their homes and families
and wished to assure themselves. Further, there were
murmurs at the extent of the losses in the front lines. No
one knew how many millions of men had laid down their
lives. There was a movement against war. Finally, while
Kerensky tried in vain to break the Austro-Hungarian line
which had been reinforced by Germany, the German counter-
attack was launched on July 19 against Tarnopol. It was

brilliantly successful. Kerensky's troops broke and fled; the whole Russian attack was disorganized. The army advanced as far as possible, but the Russians had destroyed the railway lines, which made communication a matter of grave difficulty. For the army it seemed too dangerous to attempt to reach Petrograd—there remained the navy. Threatened from their northern coast, and with a victorious German army in their country, the Russians forsook their last efforts to defy this determined foe. They asked for an armistice in November, 1917.

In Iraq the English had taken Bagdad, and the Turks had been defeated at Beersheba and Gaza, defeats that were followed by the loss of Jerusalem.

On the western front, the newly arranged German front line was strengthened as far as possible. January, February and March, 1917, passed with comparative quietness, but the month of April reopened the hostilities. On the 9th, the English attacked at Arras, the way having first been prepared by a great barrage. The English attack swept over the German defences, and carried the positions. The Germans lost many guns; their reserves failed to stand against the English, or else broke down after heroic resistance. Hindenburg was faced with another crisis; as had happened before, the English leaders did not make the fullest possible use of their victory, and this fact Hindenburg describes as "a ray of light among the many shadows of the evening of April 9." The period of relaxation did not last long. Hindenburg knew that fresh troops were already marching to the scene and that others were being brought by the railways. At the end of the conference Hindenburg shook Ludendorff's hand with the words: "Well, we have gone through worse things together than this affair of today." At Soissons the French attack, which had also started with prolonged artillery fire, was thrown back. The battle at Arras, at Soissons, and round Rheims was fought out savagely for many weeks, and the Entente had no further important success. Hindenburg's group system of defence answered the purpose for which it was designed, and the crisis was weathered again.

To the northwest of Lille, however, upon the Messines Ridge, the English started another attack. The artillery fire was severe, and the defending troops suffered more heavily than had ever been the case on previous occasions. The commanders of the army suggested it would be best to evacuate the ridge without further contest, but the occupying troops sent back the answer: "We shall hold out—we are still standing firmly." English sappers had been at work, however, and mines had been laid. On the 7th of June, the ground broke under the feet of the German soldiers and the English attack overcame the last of their resistance. Desperate efforts were made by reserves to retrieve the day, but the artillery fire was such that these could achieve no success. The German losses here were terrible and included, in addition to many valuable lives, a large number of guns and other equipment.

The autumn of 1917 caused Hindenburg to change his mind about allowing a strong attack to be made upon Italy, and he influenced the Kaiser to give his consent. The time was no more favorable to Germany that it had been the previous year; it was, in fact, more than ever a fearful risk to withdraw troops from the western front and send them to the support of Austria. What, then, made the field marshal reconsider his former decision? Simply that the Austrians had no longer the strength to resist another and expected Italian offensive, and they told Hindenburg that their front would certainly give way when this came. And, if this front gave way, the complete disintegration of the Austro-Hungarian army was threatened. The troops had fought with enthusiasm against Italy, their hereditary enemy; even men of Czecho-Slovakian race (who had been disinclined to fight Russia) did their utmost against Italy. Everything, however, had been in vain; they had been forced back upon their defences so far that Trieste was in danger of falling. It is unnecessary to dwell upon the value laid upon Trieste by the Austrians and its importance to their trade, and it is not difficult to imagine the despair with which they appealed to Hindenburg to save it. "Trieste," writes Hindenburg, "had to be saved, and, as it was not otherwise possible, by German troops."

It must be remembered that the Austrians were out-numbered almost three to one and that they had been fight-ing under conditions which Hindenburg described as being, in some ways, even more miserable than those against which the armies in France had to contend. In the Tyrolean Alps, these soldiers had heroically borne the brunt of bitter fight-ing. Hindenburg could not spare sufficient troops to make possible the tactics of encircling the Italians following a sudden descent from southern Tyrol; and he feared also that an early winter might set in before the troops could be brought from France and marched to the scene of action.

It was therefore decided to strike against the weak north flank of Cadorna's troops and then to deliver an irresistible blow to the main southern part of the Italian army.

On the 24th of October the German offensive started and was carried out with brilliant success. Cadorna, it is true, was able to bring the main part of his army to safety behind the river Piave; but he was obliged to abandon much equipment, and large numbers of prisoners fell into the hands of the Germans. English and French troops were rushed to the spot and fresh resistance was now offered. Cadorna, supported by English and French divisions, placed his left wing in the Venetian Alps; an attempt by the Germans and Austrians to dislodge them from their positions and to break the resistance of the Italians by the Piave came to nothing. Hindenburg, who had to some extent allowed himself to hope for the destruction of the Italian army, and who rejoiced at the considerable success of his soldiers, confessed nevertheless to a feeling of dissatisfaction. The great victory had not been achieved.

"It is true that our wonderful soldiers returned with justified pride from this campaign. But the joy of the soldiers is not always that of their leaders."

At the end of July, the battle in Flanders started again in all its fury. The English attacked with that dogged determination which the Germans had grown to expect from them. Hindenburg refers constantly to English *Zähigkeit*.[1] He saw in this Flanders campaign an attempt by the English to make an end of the war before American troops could be brought to France. This battle was fought upon the heavy

[1] Tenacity.

earth of Flanders, and the first line of defending troops had difficult positions to hold. Struggle succeeded struggle, every nerve was strained to the utmost, officers and men lived at the highest tension. There were heavy losses on both sides. Day succeeded day, the weeks lengthened to months, and still the fighting went on. Apparently there was no end to the English *Zähigkeit,* but the Germans, in their turn, exhibited no small measure of the same quality. They held to their posts when these were all but untenable; it seemed that nothing could dislodge them. But Hindenburg's memoirs reveal the depth of anxiety which prevailed at head-quarters. He writes that the leaders of the German armies could only pray for wet weather, which would make the heavy ground impassable, so that even the English would have to cease the offensive for a time.

The fighting continued, however, until the month of September, and there was no victory for either side. Only the vast gloom of reaction set in after the months of over-strained powers. Hindenburg, whose love of aggressive methods had now been thoroughly demonstrated, was deeply depressed by the continued defensive; not until the un-expected English attack at Cambrai was repulsed with heavy losses did he feel that there was at least a little light in the sky. At Cambrai, the English broke through the German lines with the aid of tanks, and English cavalry forced its way almost into the town. It seemed that the day was lost, when fresh German troops hurried to the spot and made a wholly successful flank attack. They were able to regain from the English practically all they had lost and to emerge victorious. Hindenburg himself found a very special pleasure in this victory, for it was the first that had been won since he had taken over the leadership of the armies, and it was the result, too, of the first considerable attack by Germans since that event. Its effect upon the morale of the army was very great, and the fact that it had followed immediately upon an attack with tanks reduced to a certain extent the sense of helplessness and terror which the infantrymen experience in face of the invulnerable new weapon. Hindenburg felt sure that the ingenuity of his technical experts would soon find means of combating this monster of modern warfare, which produced so annihilating an effect upon a mere man.

The French supported the endeavors of England by an offensive at Verdun and another near Soissons in October. At both these places Germany was well defended and the attackers had again to report heavy losses. For the most part, however, the French remained quiet.

The situation of the Bulgarian armies on the Macedonian front remained unchanged through the summer of 1917. Sarrail did not engage in much fighting, and so Bulgaria simply remained where it was. At this time, however, its chief trouble was not so much the attacks from Sarrail's army as the mobilization of the Greeks. Hindenburg paid little attention to this anxiety, for he did not believe that Greece would ever succeed in raising an army capable of taking the field, and the reports he received confirmed this view. In this, time was to prove him correct, and he set down Bulgaria's anxiety to a recollection of the events of 1913.

The defeats of Turkey in Palestine and the loss of Jerusalem were matters that troubled Hindenburg very deeply, and it was with considerable relief that he heard of the curious apathy with which the news was greeted in Constantinople. He had expected riots and excitement, for he did not believe that Jerusalem could ever be recaptured. When, instead of violent outbreaks, only indifference was manifested, he felt that another crisis had been surmounted.

In February, 1917, the Kaiser decided to move his head-quarters from Pless to Kreuznach, in order to be nearer to the French front, and in consequence of the desire of the Emperor of Austria to be in intimate touch both with his minister and with his military headquarters, which were set up at Baden near Vienna at the beginning of the year.

Hindenburg left Pless with some regrets, for the owners of neighboring estates had been very hospitable to the army officers. He could not often, at this time, enjoy his favorite sport of deer-stalking, for his time was fully occupied with more serious matters, but he had been able occasionally to accept one of the many invitations showered upon him by people of the neighborhood.

In Kreuznach, however, he found a very warm welcome awaiting him from people who remembered his former con-nection with the Rhine country as chief of the General Staff of the 8th Army Corps. He was already acquainted with the town and he relates how its inhabitants vied with one another in showing their pleasure at his return to their land. The home of the General Staff and their dining-room were daily decked with flowers by Rhineland *Mädels,*[1] who were eager to honor the aged field marshal and to show him that they appreciated to the full his great triumphs on many fields of

[1] Girls.

battle. The victor of Tannenberg was no every-day being, but he writes that he accepted the homage offered him as an honor to the whole army, of which he was one of the oldest representatives.

In Kreuznach, he celebrated his seventieth birthday. The first person to offer him congratulations was the Kaiser, who made a special journey to Hindenburg's quarters. This constituted Hindenburg's greatest joy in the occasion. The day was bright, and the autumn sun shone upon the faces of the children of Kreuznach who turned out to offer him their good wishes. Many wounded soldiers appeared on the same errand, as well as some veterans who had fought with him upon other battlegrounds, the memory of which had been eclipsed by the Homeric struggle of the later day. Hindenburg relates a little event which took place on the night of his birthday. After he had gone to bed, the anti-aircraft guns started to fire with vigor, and did not cease until they had exhausted their ammunition. There had been rumors of an enemy air-raid, and it seemed that the gun crews had started to fire on a false alarm. Hindenburg, who knew that the ammunition would give out quickly, breathed a sigh of relief to realize that when this occurred he would at last be able to sleep. The next morning the Kaiser showed him a number of shell splinters, from German guns, which had landed in the garden of his quarters. There had, after all, been some little danger in the night—but a large section of the population had believed that the guns were being fired in honor of Hindenburg's birthday.

Meanwhile, political questions had become acute, and the domestic condition of the countries allied to Germany was such that they had to have other than military assistance. In Turkey there was danger of starvation. No one had sufficient food; this was not because of a blockade such as that from which Germany was suffering, but because there was no organization and no proper transport. Somehow the needs of the army were supplied and somehow the population in the towns were provided with bare necessaries. Germany had to send bread to Constantinople and to arrange for grain to be despatched to Turkey from Roumania. This help was provided, in spite of the terrible conditions in Germany because, as Hindenburg states, the people of Constantinople would otherwise have starved. Had they suffered in this way, they would have revolted and Turkish military assistance, which she continued to afford in spite of all her trials, would have been lost to Germany. In Asia Minor the Turkish army was daily growing smaller owing to the astonishing number of deserters, which amounted to hundreds of thousands. Even this, however, did not cause Turkey to abandon the situation, and she did what was required of her with her depleted forces.

In Bulgaria, the country of rich harvests, there was also distress, owing to crops that were little more than moderate. Germany suggested that the crops should be evenly distributed in all districts, when they would have sufficed, but the answer was: "We don't understand these affairs!" It was only too true, and there was no strong leader to take this helpless population in hand and show it how to deal with its own affairs. A leader was needed; but there was none, and the country was torn by many political factions. The majority raised trouble over the home policy of the government. The army began to suffer from lack of supplies, and the general discontent spread to the ranks of the army. Germany made many suggestions for the improvement of the domestic affairs of the country but, although they received some recognition, there was no one to see that they were put into force. Worse than the food question in Bulgaria was the mistrust with which Germany began to be regarded both in Sofia and in the country at large. Doubt was expressed regarding the ability, or even the willingness, of Germany to fulfil all the promises she had made to her smaller ally. The German government had to do all it could to meet any demands made by Bulgaria and to keep the support of the army.

In Austria-Hungary, matters went from bad to worse. The efforts made by the government to obtain some kind of peace between the different races which dwelt in the country failed completely. A powerful move had been made by the Church to unite the country by means of a religious bond; this, too, failed entirely. Racial prejudice was brought more strongly into the foreground by the uneven distribution of food. One town went hungry, while another had plenty; and those who had sufficient to eat were completely indifferent to the sufferings of their neighbors. Disbelief in the possibility of winning the war daily spread like a blight over the country and the faction that desired peace at any price increased. The victory over the Italians gave no pleasure to the hungry population, and the news of the breakdown of Russia was received with indifference. Hindenburg saw that it would not be long before the Austrian government would have to yield to the demands for peace: he did not care to consider

what the result would be should the government un-
expectedly find power to resist the will of the people in this
matter.

In Germany itself, serious difficulties and dissensions had
arisen, notably between the government and the military
leaders. Hindenburg, whose chief care was the army, was
determined that the full resources of his country should be
placed at the disposal of the fighting forces. He saw with
deepening distress how the unity of the country was disappearing, and he realized that this would have a weakening
effect upon the army. He found himself in strong opposition
to the government, and in July he handed in his resignation
to the Kaiser. This was not accepted, but the Lord Chancellor's (Bethmann Hollweg's) request to resign was duly
approved. The retirement of Bethmann Hollweg was directly
followed by the outward revelation of the thinly disguised
hostility which existed between the various political parties,
and it was soon seen that the majority was in the hands of
the Left.

Dr. Michaelis, who succeeded Bethmann Hollweg, was
able to remain only a short time in office; circumstances
proved too much for him and he was obliged to lay down
the difficult post which he had so fearlessly accepted.

Hindenburg writes sadly that the real seriousness of Germany's situation was forgotten by the people at home, who
lost sight of everything but party interests and dogmas. He
was right in feeling that the lack of unity at home would
have a bad effect upon the soldiers; but he forgot that
people who have given everything, who have made supreme
sacrifices, are bound to reach a point where they can do no

more. The sufferings and deeds of the army obscured for him the sufferings and deeds of those who had had to stay behind. In his memoirs, he gives weight to the effect which prolonged starvation must produce upon any population, but he does not seem to give it full weight. He emphasizes perpetually the necessity of keeping the army in the best shape possible, but he nowhere emphasizes the pressing necessity of a proper administration of home affairs.

A new chancellor was found in Graf Hertling, and it was hoped that he would be able to lead the country effectively. He showed great skill in the way he handled the different parties and, although he exhibited some distrust towards the leaders of the army, he was honored by Hindenburg for the gallant way he had answered his country's call in his old age. He remained in office until just before the Armistice was signed, when he retired. His death occurred shortly after his resignation.

Hindenburg refers with disgust to the propaganda which was used by the enemy to increase the dissatisfaction that was spreading among the German people. "This type of propaganda," he writes, "was called 'enlightening the enemy.' It should have been called 'veiling the truth' and, even worse, 'poisoning the spirit of the enemy.' It arises from a knowledge of insufficient strength to meet and overcome an opponent in open, honorable fight and inability to break down his moral strength by a bravely wielded sword."

Whether such propaganda is a justifiable means of fighting may be open to discussion, but one thing is abundantly clear. It could be effective only when the country was already disunited. Any process of "enlightening the enemy" or even of "poisoning the spirit of the enemy" would glance harmlessly off the armor of perfect unity and firm national will. But Germany has never had, and has not even now achieved, complete internal harmony and there is an absence of national will. Before the war the regimentation which was inculcated in every grade of society and the two years of military service welded the huge population into some semblance of unity. The monarchy was the pivotal point upon which even that semblance turned. Now, in 1917, the Socialists and the extremists began to murmur audibly and to ask where the monarchy had led them. Anti-war broadsheets were sold in the streets and pacifist meetings became frequent. The soldiers, returning on leave after months of soul-shattering warfare in the trenches, began to be infected with the spirit that prevailed at home. Not every man found himself in agreement with it, nor even nearly every man, but all the soldiers knew of its existence and this had some demoralizing results. A man who knows that a sullen and discontented home lies at his back and a strong and determined foe is before him cannot fight with the same enthusiasm as when his struggles are supported and applauded by his countrymen.

In the face of these facts, the achievements both of the German military leaders and of the army during the year 1918 were all the more remarkable.

Hindenburg tells how the French prisoners spoke of the misery existing in their country and of the food distress that was beginning to be felt at home. "But," he writes, "their own appearance did not support these words." Of the English prisoners, he says: "They talked at the end of 1917 as they had at the end of 1914. None of them enjoyed the war, but in England this was not the main consideration. Demands were simply made, and fulfilled."

Hindenburg continually praises the heroism of his armies, their enthusiasm, their joy in battle and work, and deplores the absence of political talent among his countrymen. "The lack of political discipline, which has become second nature to the Englishman, and the absence of a patriotism un-alloyed by cosmopolitan ideas, such as burned in the hearts of the French, were to blame, in my opinion, for the Peace Resolutions which met with the approval of the Government in July, 1917."

CHAPTER XI

THE year 1918 was to be the decisive one, and Hindenburg believed that it would be possible for Germany to wrest a victory from the Allies. With the release of the forces on the eastern frontier, the Germans in France would outnumber the Allies, and a determined attack could be made at one part of the line without weakening the defences of 1917. True, the Allies had more guns and very many more airplanes than Germany could muster, but, if well-seasoned reinforcements could reach the western front before the fresh strength from America could make itself felt, there was hope of victory. How could that hope exist?

"The answer," says Hindenburg, "is easy to give but difficult to explain; it is expressed in the word *trust*. Not trust in a lucky star or in vague hopes, still less trust in numbers or in outward strength; but the trust that enables a leader to place his troops before the fire of an enemy with complete confidence that they will endure to the utmost and make possible the apparently impossible. It was this trust that carried me through 1916-17."

Further, the soldiers in France would certainly welcome the chance of an offensive. For years they had lain hidden in foul and muddy trenches and suffered death and wounds from artillery. The enemy went "over the top" every now and then, and all that the Germans could do was to defend their positions. Small wonder that they were sick to death of these conditions. Death was easier to face in the heat and storm of attack than in the dismal trenches. Hindenburg would find that the right spirit ruled when he gave his orders.

Hindenburg hoped not only that the military situation would be saved, but that there would be a brighter outlook on the political horizon. A victory would surely, so he argued, cause the civil population to cease their complaints and tears. It would show them that the hardships of the past years had not been in vain, and that their leaders could recognize the favorable moment and turn it to the best advantage.

He attached great importance to destroying the military pretensions of Russia and Roumania, and to this end he exhorted the Austrians to maintain their fronts. He was convinced that this would not be a matter of any serious difficulty to them. He knew Bulgaria to be strong enough to stand up against her opponents in Macedonia. The Turks had been freed from some of their troubles by the Russian breakdown in Asia Minor, and he believed they could advance their fortunes in Mesopotamia and Syria with the armies released from Asia Minor.

Hindenburg now laid his plans for the offensive, and he chose that part of the line which stretched from Arras through Cambrai and St.-Quentin to La Fère. Hindenburg writes that he chose to move against the English because their offensives had revealed an inability to cope with swiftly changing situations, and he suspected that like weaknesses would be found in their methods of defence. "They worked too much according to scheme."

The headquarters of the German General Staff were now removed from Kreuznach to Spa. An additional advance headquarters was set up at Avesnes, and there the greater part of the General Staff arrived on March 19, to discuss plans. Hindenburg was impressed by the absence of changes in France, and he was almost able to think himself back again in 1870. Now, as then, the inhabitants sat in their doorways, "the men silent, the women voluble, controlling the conversation; the children playing and singing on the green, as if in the midst of most profound peace. Happy youth!" Once again, as in the former war with France, Hindenburg found much to admire in the attitude of the French population. The Kaiser did not take up quarters in Avesnes but lived in his special train, which was moved from place to place as the fortunes of war changed. He spent much of his time with the army and took little thought for his own comfort and safety.

The attack was planned to open on March 21. The fair spring weather suddenly changed; rain set in. But Hindenburg welcomed the clouds and storms. They served somewhat as a cloak to veil the final preparations, the approach of the reserves and the drawing of guns to the required positions. No one knew whether news of the intended offensive had reached the English, but the moment approached without any unusual activity from the enemy. The excitement rose with every hour; soldiers and their leaders were drawn together in the common hope that the laurels of victory were at last within their grasp. The

20th of March came, and with it increasingly unfavorable weather conditions. Wind and rain enveloped the country-side, but it was resolved not to allow any postponement.

March 21 dawned and the land was covered with a thick mist. In Avesnes, the General Staff heard the distant rolling of the guns, which had spoken incessantly from the early morning hours. The German artillery was answered by that of the Allied troops, but this seemed to be mostly range-finding.

Still on the morning of March 21, it was not possible to know whether or not the English were prepared for the approaching storm. At 10 o'clock, the German infantry left the trenches and charged into the dense mist upon their opponents. Hindenburg waited anxiously for news. Reports reached him and were contradicted immediately by following despatches. The position, on the whole, seemed hopeful. Towards midday the fog began to disperse and the sun shone down upon a scene or slaughter and bitter contention. Almost everywhere the English front line had been captured, but when evening set in, it was seen that the centre of the German army and the right-wing group had been stopped at the second line of defence. The left wing, however, had pushed rapidly forward at St.-Quentin, where there was a weaker defending force. Hindenburg, satisfied with the results achieved, was not inclined to rejoice too soon—the second day might easily produce a setback and the German offensive might suffer the fate that had befallen so many Allied attacks. The evening of the second day came, and Hindenburg was able to feel that his trust both in the methods he had employed and in the ability of his troops to move forward with skill and rapidity had been fully justified. The centre of the German offensive had taken the third line of defence, the left wing had moved westward with a speed which had not been expected of them. The right wing had forced the English to evacuate their second line of defence, but had not been able to press forward sufficiently to make possible the destruction of the English in occupation of the Cambrai sector. Many enemy guns and great stores of ammunition and equipment had fallen into the hands of the victors, and files of prisoners began to pass down the white roads to captivity.

March 23 saw the advance of the centre of the German army and the development of the movement of the left wing further westward. The Somme was reached, and, at one point, forded. The first German shells fell in Paris. The German right wing, however, could not advance beyond the English second line of defence. English *Zähigkeit* was serving its purpose once more, and the fierce attacks could not prevail against it. Hindenburg now determined to make the utmost strategic use of the advance, and he considered that the town of Amiens would be the best central point to attack, because of its railways and because it was a principal junction between the armies of France and England. If Amiens could be captured, a dividing line could be drawn between the forces of these two allies, and he believed that such separation would affect their relationship: it might serve to define the difference in the political interests of the two countries. And so the Germans advanced upon Amiens. But England and France saw the danger that threatened them, and English reinforcements from the north and many

French troops were brought to the spot. Amiens must not be allowed to fall.

The German forces marched on across the old battle-fields of the Somme, over the shell-holed country that had been the scene of so much spilt blood and such nerve-racking terror. On they swept, and the town of Bapaume fell into their hands. The English, their resistance broken, retreated raggedly upon Amiens. There seemed to be a real possibility that German soldiers might reach this town. The right wing, however, was unable to advance against the English and it became necessary to attack the hills to the east of Arras in order to help this part of the line. This attempt was only partly successful. Now the centre of the German attack had to meet French reinforcements, and Hindenburg's hope that Amiens would be taken, or at least that Villers-Bretonneux (from whence it might be shelled) would fall, was proved vain. Even German soldiers had been unable to achieve the impossible. Men are human beings and strength cannot be kept up indefinitely. Hindenburg, however, refused to admit that the effort had failed and that the aim might not still be attained. The infantry was given the rest it needed; and early in April another attempt was made to capture Villers-Bretonneux. This was also unsuccessful and the offensive was repulsed with considerable loss. Amiens was shelled by German artillery but it remained safely in the hands of the Allies.

On the 9th of April the Germans started their offensive in Flanders. They attacked along the front from Armentières to La Bassée, and were obliged to make their way over broad fields still wet and soft from months of rain.

They ploughed through the morass and their advance was covered by a powerful barrage. Along this front were placed some Portuguese troops, and when these saw the Germans approaching them across apparently impassable country, they forsook their positions and fled in great disorder. On April 10 Estaires was won by the Germans, who were able to get possession also of much ground to the north of Armentières. On April 11 Armentières was evacuated by the English troops. The offensive went forward, Bailleul was captured, and the Germans were able to reach the hills.

The movements of the German troops were seriously hampered by the great difficulty of communicating with their supplies. Over the soaking, swampy fields came the ammunition, but in insufficient quantities. Had it not been for the stores abandoned by the English it would even have been impossible to feed the troops adequately.

In the meantime, the German infantry was subjected to a raking machine-gun fire and the situation became daily more critical. Retreat meant certain disaster, and attack— at a time when attack was very dangerous—seemed to be the only hope of salvation. Mount Kemmel, which had always been in the hands of the Allies and which was strongly fortified, seemed to Hindenburg to offer a good aim for the shaft of the attack. "We hoped that the external appearance of this hill was stronger than its real tactical strength." On the 25th of April the storming of the hill was undertaken, the English defence was broken down immediately, and the Germans were left undisputed masters of the field. Ypres was threatened and the English prepared to defend it to the last ounce of their strength. Hindenburg's immediate objective, however, was not Ypres but Cassel, to the end that German heavy artillery might be able to shell Calais and Boulogne. The news he received from the Flanders front was good: here and there, it was true, the troops might have failed, but in the main he had some reason for his high hopes. By the end of April, however, these were dashed. French troops arrived to the support of the English and in May there was nothing to be done but to fall back upon the defensive.

The German leaders now turned their attention from Flanders to France, and, on May 27, another great offensive was made between Soissons and Rheims. This attack was attended by astonishing success, and Hindenburg writes that on the afternoon of the first day the report which reached the High Command stated that the German infantry was already crossing the Aisne. In a few days the Marne from Château-Thierry to Dormans had been taken. The north wing of the attacking army approached Villers-Cotterêts, and Rheims was threatened. Everywhere the French were driven back and they abandoned an enormous quantity of stores and ammunition.

About this time, Hindenburg visited personally the battle-fields near Laon. In the winter of 1917, this town had scarcely been disturbed, but Hindenburg had an opportunity to see what terrible havoc had been wrought in the mean-time. Paris had been shelled by long-distance guns in the neighborhood of Laon, and subsequently the French had shelled this town heavily, believing that enemy ammunition was being brought there. Hindenburg writes that many inhabitants had been unable to escape and had been obliged to hide themselves in their cellars to avoid destruction. They were in great misery and distress, but the Germans were powerless to help them. Laon was, of course, not the only town that suffered bombardment; but it certainly was one of the worst sufferers. The field marshal, on seeing the terribly changed aspect of the town and the fear of the people, confessed that it was a hard spectacle for a soldier to have to contemplate; and he also felt great compassion toward the columns of prisoners, in connection with which he tells a story in his *Aus meinem Leben*. One day he stood with another high officer of the German army in the village of St.-Quentin when a number of prisoners were marched down the street. His companion stepped up to the guard and called a halt, after which he addressed the row of shamed-looking men. He told them how the Germans honored the conduct of the troops opposing them and added that captivity often fell to the lot of those who had held out the longest. Hindenburg writes that the effect of these words was tremendous and in particular that a tall young man, whose head had hung in shame, suddenly raised it and gazed gratefully at the speaker of these comforting words—in whom he recognized the Kaiser.

In the meantime the offensive was driven onwards along the front from Montdidier to Noyon, in the direction of Compiègne. It was impossible, however, to reach this town and again an attempt to take Villers-Cotterêts was unsuccessful. Hindenburg was forced to admit that his troops did not possess the strength to break through the principal part of the defending army which was massed here. The Soissons-Rheims offensive had, however, been successful beyond the highest expectations and gave rise to further hopes of ultimate victory, though these were never to be fulfilled.

Although the chief part of the French Reserve Army was ranged round Compiègne and Villers-Cotterêts, the railway service was so excellent and so well organized that any threatened part of the front could immediately receive support. At the beginning of July, strong American detachments were expected and it did not seem to Hindenburg likely that the French would take the offensive before these arrived. In the neighborhood of Rheims was also a strong force, composed not only of French, but also of English and Italians. Hindenburg decided to take the initiative, and on July 15 the German guns thundered their new barrage. Round Rheims, a terrific struggle blazed into action, although the town itself was not immediately threatened. The German infantry stormed and took the first line of trenches and then endeavored to carry their attack into the second. Here, however, they met with powerful resistance and a devastating fire from the French artillery. The German supporting batteries were brought up, and Hindenburg writes that these had actually to be dragged to the scene of action by soldiers, because the terror-stricken horses refused to advance over the fields which were full of shell-holes. The German guns, brought with such difficulty to their emplacements, were destroyed almost immediately by the enemy. To the southwest of Rheims, and on both banks of the Marne, the German soldiers succeeded in pressing forward, especially in the direction of Épernay, where they had to meet a determined resistance, which they were able for the most part to overcome.

By the evening of the 15th of July, Hindenburg was able once more to commend the courage and ability of the German army. Along the whole attacking front something like fifty guns had been taken, and more than a thousand prisoners were marched to the rear. Here was no small success, but Hindenburg was not entirely satisfied and he waited anxiously for greater successes on the following day. But July 16 reached its close, and it had to be admitted that the troops had nowhere advanced to any considerable extent. It seemed that it would be better to cease the offensive in Champagne for fear that the troops might suffer such heavy losses as would make them unable to sustain even a defensive action. Hindenburg, who saw that no further gains could be expected, gave his consent to the cessation of attack and the resumption of purely defensive methods. To the south of the Marne, however, and in the hills round about Rheims, it was possible to continue the German offensive. North of the river the offensive had almost ceased, and here, too, it was eventually necessary to take the defensive. On both banks of the river the Germans pressed slowly on in the direction of Épernay, and the evening of the 16th found them only about six miles from the town.

The 17th of July dawned and the battle in Champagne grew quieter. The guns continued to speak, it is true, but the sorely pressed German infantry was able to enjoy some breathing space. To the south of the Marne, under continuous attack by the Allies, the Germans were scarcely able to defend the ground they had won, and in places they were obliged to retreat, although Hindenburg was deeply distressed by the necessity. In the hills the Allied attacks were so fierce that the German troops had the greatest difficulty in keeping their positions. An advance here was out of the question.

On the 18th of July came a blow from the Allies. German soldiers who could be spared for the work had gone to the harvesting in the wheatfields. Suddenly shells began raining down, but the Germans noticed that their own artillery was replying only half-heartedly. The whole country-side was covered with mist. Shortly after the artillery fire had started, the clatter of machine guns began to be heard and before the German soldiers had had time to realize what was happening, they saw the dreaded tanks rolling towards them through the waving wheatfields. The Allies had attacked upon the whole front between the Aisne and the Marne, and the front line had already been broken through in several places. The men who remained in the shattered front-line trenches fought desperately and the supports in the rear endeavored to form an adequate line of defence. But the heroism exhibited by these troops could not save the day. The Allies broke through all along that section of the front. The German right-wing troops were obliged to abandon Château-Thierry, although they were able, to some extent, to preserve their position on the Marne.

The situation had now, however, become more than serious. Time after time the German front threatened to break —the soldiers had already done their utmost and were equal to no further effort. Hindenburg writes:

We must leave the Marne. . . . How the enemy will rejoice if, for the second time, the name "Marne" is connected with a turning point in the history of the war! Paris, indeed all France, will

[137]

breathe again; this news will affect the whole world! . . . But now the military point of view only must be considered. Its demand is clear and simple: out of this situation! . . . Although General Foch throws all his strength upon us from every side, so far he has only here and there achieved a deep penetration of our lines. Step by step, therefore, we are able to retreat. We can draw our valuable stores out of reach of the enemy and we can take up our posts in an orderly manner in the new line of defence.

Those divisions intended for the attack in Flanders had to be hurried to the support of the soldiers by the Marne; and Hindenburg writes that this was the worst of the situation. It was now impossible to make an offensive against the English, for there were neither troops nor *matériel.*

The 8th of August was a bad day for Germany. Fog hung heavily over the land, and in the morning news came to headquarters that the English had broken the German lines at Peronne. In the neighborhood of Amiens tanks had forced their way past the defences. Many Germans were saved by the command to lie still in the wheatfields. The grain had not been cut, and, although the risk of remaining still was great, it was taken, and the concealed soldiers were not discovered by their opponents. Against this attack, the Germans for the moment were powerless to act. Rumor, an evil that none can combat, maintained that English cavalry had already reached and was threatening the rear.

Once again, however, failure by the Allies to press forward and make the best possible use of the advantage gained helped the Germans in their extremity. The afternoon of August 8 was almost quiet and the night uneventful. Through the darkness swept the trains bearing supports to the stricken front, but the counter-attack made by the Germans on the 9th of August was a failure and many lives were lost.

In spite of the gravity of the military situation, Hindenburg still hoped to save the day. On August 13 he attended a consultation at Spa, when the government discussed affairs with the military leaders. Hindenburg admitted that things were not well with the army, but he pointed out that the Germans were still holding miles of French soil and that this fact must not be forgotten. The chancellor, Graf Hertling, expressed the view that an official offer of peace should not be made by Germany until the military situation had improved.

The days passed, and on August 20 the French again broke the German lines between the Oise and the Aisne, after three days of severe fighting. On August 26, the English advanced at Arras with some success, and on the 2nd of September, a great German retreat had to be undertaken both in France and in Flanders.

While the Germans were thus being forced to retreat along the west front, serious news was brought to the High Command. Bulgaria collapsed. The country, which for long had been torn by opposing political factions within, was suffering from hunger and general disorganization. Even the army was so badly fed and clothed that mutinies were frequent, and that section of the population which wanted peace increased daily and grew more vociferous. The soldiers simply left the battlefields, and the centre part of the army made little or no attempt to face the English offensive of September. A few German officers and men did what they could to arrest the rot that had set in, but in vain.

The Bulgarians, writes Hindenburg, suddenly said that they were tired of fighting and wanted to go home to their wives and children. The officers did what they could to encourage the men to hold out against the comparatively weak divisions of English and Serbians. Hindenburg even quotes cases in which the Bulgarians assisted the Germans to bring guns into position and to prepare for action and then hurriedly disappeared, leaving the actual fighting to the Germans. So impossible were the conditions, for those who were trying to offer assistance, that Hindenburg and his staff sent troops from the western front and agreed to dispense, for the time being, with the services there of those Austro-Hungarian divisions that could otherwise have been sent to France; these divisions also were now hurried to the Macedonian front. The supports, however, arrived too late, and Bulgaria signed an armistice on the 29th of September.

In the meantime, the German troops on the western front held on. It was all they could do, and even that seemed too much to ask of them. Hindenburg and his staff were now faced with the question: "When must we come to an end?" Hindenburg writes:

He who, in such a case, turns for a solution to the great mistress of humanity, History, hears nothing of caution, but of boldness. When I turn for example to our greatest monarch, I receive the reply: "Hold on!"

In the meantime, while the gallant army was spending the last of its strength in vain endeavor against a stronger power, the political horizon grew darker and darker. The reserves who came from home brought to an army already at bay tales of imminent revolution. If the people at home

GENERAL VON HINDENBURG, CANDIDATE FOR THE REICHSBLOCK,
REVIEWS A DEMONSTRATION OF PATRIOTIC ASSOCIATIONS AT HIS
VILLA IN HANOVER

could not hold out, how should the men in the trenches? But even through these bitter hours, they fought on.

At the end of September, the Kaiser returned to Germany and on the 1st of October Hindenburg followed him. As he writes:—"I hoped to fight pessimism and to restore trust. But the inward disturbances proved too heavy to make it possible to achieve this aim." Things dragged on miserably through the month of October and the rift between the statesmen and the soldiers widened until it became impassable. Hindenburg, however, directed the following letter to the new chancellor, Prince Max of Baden, on October 24:—

I am unable to conceal from your Highness that, at the last discussion of the government, I painfully missed an appeal for goodwill and for the army.

I had hoped that the new government would gather the whole strength of the German nation into the service of the defence of the Fatherland. This has not occurred. On the contrary, with little exception, reconciliation has been spoken of rather than defence of the Fatherland against the threatening foe. This has first depressed and now disturbed the army, as is proved by serious symptoms.

To assure the national defence, the soldiers require not only leaders but also the spirit of conviction that it is necessary to fight and the mental buoyancy which must support them in their high enterprise.

Your Highness must surely agree with me that, considering the vast importance of the morale of the soldiers, of the government officials, and of the people's representatives, this spirit must be borne into and held upright in the army and the people.

I appeal to your Highness as head of the new government to be true to this sacred task.

This letter had no effect. The chancellor, instead, demanded that Ludendorff be removed from his post because

the leaders of the army had interfered in political matters.
The Kaiser felt that he would have to support the cabinet
and the chancellor, and when on October 25 both Ludendorff and Hindenburg handed in their resignations, he
accepted the former's, but he asked Hindenburg to stay with
the army.

Here was a bitter tragedy! After so many years of struggling side by side, these two men were to be parted by
politics—those politics of which Hindenburg had so often
to complain. In his memoirs, he writes only a few curt
sentences, but they do not serve to conceal how deeply he
felt this blow.

It was too late. Politics demanded sacrifices; the first was offered
up on October 26. On the evening of that day, I left Berlin, where
I had gone with my First Quartermaster-General to consult with
our supreme War Lord, and returned to my headquarters. I was
alone. His Majesty had approved General Ludendorff's request
to resign and had refused me a similar request. On the following
day I entered the rooms where, up to the present, we had worked
together. I felt as if I had returned to the deserted house after
attending the funeral of some one especially dear to me.

Through all the days of political uncertainty and difficulty,
through all the increasing danger signals that were to be
noted at home, the army held their own in France. Forced
as they were to make a harrowing retreat over ground they
had so hardly won, they still fought on, defending, retreating, and dying. If the army could hold out (and Hindenburg believed that the enemy could be kept from German
soil for many months yet) and if the population would support its endeavors, the government might still gain an honorable peace. If, however, the deadly spirit of revolution

should grip either people or army, then indeed everything would be lost.

On November 9, chaos broke loose. Hindenburg, seeing the throne threatened and the great work of Bismarck about to be overthrown, expressed his determination to send the army to fight the revolutionaries. He did not believe that these were backed by the will of the people. His soldiers should turn away from the enemy without and fight the enemy within. But General Groener, successor to Ludendorff, pressed upon his chief the objections of the rest of the General Staff and showed strong proof that the army would not train its guns upon its own people. An attempt to force soldiers into a civil war would result only in mutiny; it was useless to think of such procedure. Hindenburg was obliged to agree, for the proofs that his plan would be even worse than useless were too strong to be disregarded.

Serious riots took place in Berlin, which the government was powerless to stop. Thousands of sailors who had helped to hoist the red flag of revolution upon their battleships had thronged to the capital. Soldiers who were in reserve calmly sold their equipment and made for their homes.

In the middle of the tumult and distraction the Kaiser's advisers recommended him to take refuge in Holland, and he expressed his willingness to do all that lay in his power, even to abdicate, to save the country. And on this fateful 9th of November, Prince Max of Baden announced the abdication of the Kaiser before the latter had made any decision. It was also announced that the Crown Prince had renounced his claim to his father's throne. A few hours after this momentous news had been made known Scheidemann (the Secretary of State) proclaimed the German Republic.

The Kaiser decided that he would stay with the army, though he could not remain its commander-in-chief. This position he gave over to Hindenburg, the man whom he could trust. Even then, in that hour of gloom, the old field marshal stood faithfully at his post; even then, when he might have found good reasons for leaving it. But the cold star of duty which had guided him through the whole of his long life illumined his path—and he remained. The Kaiser, however, finally gave way to the pressure of his advisers and crossed the boundary of Holland, and he was followed by the Crown Prince. Hindenburg had gone to bed on the 9th of November after receiving a message that the Kaiser would remain at his side. On the morning of the 10th, he awoke to find himself alone, for urgent counsels had changed the monarch's mind and he had fled. He had released the army from its oath of fealty and had left to one old man the superhuman task of taking the soldiers back to their country.

At the present day, it is impossible to judge whether it might or might not have made all the difference to Germany had the Emperor not left his country. His motives for doing so were doubtless high, but it is open to question whether he was rightly served by those about him. A stronger king, a true descendant of Frederick the Great, would surely have stayed with his army, for there can be little question that a large part of the soldiery would have stood by him. Some German historians express the view that even at the eleventh hour the Revolution could have been stopped (though at the cost of some bloodshed) had the

Kaiser acted with vigor. It is only fair to say that others believe that the Revolution would have triumphed in any case.

Though released from his oath of loyalty to the Kaiser, Hindenburg could not help feeling bound to the monarch he had served with such devotion and faith. When he found that he was quite alone and that he would have to submit to a government with which he could have no sympathy, all his inclination must have been to resign. He knew, however, that he alone could hope to have any success in getting the troops peacefully back to Germany and to their homes, and he conquered his desire to withdraw from his responsibility. He revealed the true greatness of his personality when he placed himself and his authority at the service of the Social Democrat, Friedrich Ebert, to whom and to whose associates Prince Max of Baden handed over the reins of power. This act represented the supreme self-sacrifice; it revealed the extent of Hindenburg's love for his country and his people as nothing else could have done. More than once he had shown that he was a great soldier; he now proved that he was also a very great man. The Entente demanded that the occupied country should be evacuated in fifteen days, and in fifteen days more the evacuation of the left bank of the Rhine was to be completed. This task placed a terrific strain upon the High Command and upon the war-weary soldiers. Three million men had to be conveyed home along streets which for the most part were uphill. The railways were so badly disorganized that the greater part of the army had to move on foot. It must also be remembered that among those three million were many thousands of men who were wounded or ill, and this fact added to the difficulties of the task. It was, however, carried out with that perfect organization which is the just pride of Germany; and, for the most part, it was carried out peacefully. The men whose heroism had won admiration in the ranks of the enemy remained true to their training to the end. With every opportunity of turning into a "red" army of terror, they nevertheless refrained from mutiny and pillage and carried their laurels untarnished into the quiet of their homes. They followed with honor the great example of duty which had been set them by Hindenburg.

For the most part—but not entirely. In Berlin there were fierce street fights, and the Revolution—as most other revolutions have done—took its toll of lives. At last the fighting came to an end, and it was now the task of every man who had the weal of the Fatherland at heart to help to stem the tide of Bolshevism.

Finally the day came when the Allies demanded the German assent or refusal to the Versailles terms. Hindenburg was asked for an opinion. He replied that he did not think that a resumption of military activities could possibly lead to a good result, but that to a soldier a death with honor was preferable to a shameful peace. The German government, however, yielded to the demands of the Allies—it is certainly difficult to see what else they could have done—and the soldier had to bow to the strong hand of fate. Against one clause, however, he set himself with fierce determination: the person of the Kaiser should never be handed over to the Allies. On the 3rd of July, Hindenburg wrote a letter to President Ebert in which he assumed the full responsibility for all the actions of the High Command from August, 1916, including the orders of the Kaiser, which he declared had been given in every case on his personal advice.

On the same date he directed the following letter to Marshal Foch:

As a soldier old in service and for a time the principal military adviser of my Emperor and King, I consider it my duty to address these lines, in the name of the old German Army, to you, Sir Generalissimo, as Chief of the Armies of the Allied Powers, to ask you to refrain from demanding that His Majesty the Kaiser be delivered into your hands. As the supreme head of an army which through centuries has upheld as its highest ideal the tradition of true soldiers' honor and knightly sentiment, you will be able to appreciate our feelings. I am ready to make every sacrifice to keep this shameful humiliation from our people and our name. Therefore, I put my person entirely at the disposal of the Allied Powers, in the place of my royal master. I am convinced that every other officer of the old army would be prepared to do the same.

This letter was vouchsafed no reply.

On the day upon which it was written, July 3, Hindenburg laid down his office and returned to the quiet of his house at Hanover. At last, it seemed, he would be able to live in peace and retirement and to spend the remaining years of his life in the intimate home circle which meant so much to him.

Even then, however, though he did not know it, his work for the Fatherland had not been completed: he was destined before very long to be called to the highest position which the new Germany had to offer.

CHAPTER XII

ON July 4, 1919, Hindenburg reached the town of Hanover which had prepared a festive welcome for its hero. The streets were hung with flags and garlanded with foliage and flowers, and all the inhabitants lined the pavements to join in the cries of welcome. Hanover had been the first town of many to present him with its keys, and the citizens now placed a house at his disposal which was to be his for life. The famous painting of Hindenburg and Ludendorff at work by Professor Vogel had also been acquired by the town.

The field marshal was not, however, to be allowed to enjoy the retirement he craved. Fame surrounded him and set him so much apart that he could not even walk in the early mornings without being followed by a crowd. "My wife," he said to a visitor on one occasion, "has gone shopping. I used to like to do this myself, but now if I go out there is always danger that I shall cause a traffic block because of the crowds that follow me!" Had he been physically a smaller man, he might have escaped attention to some extent, but his giant figure attracted every eye.

On October 2, his birthday, his house was besieged by admirers and stormed by the school children. As often as he would consent to appear they cheered him and sang the *"Deutschland über alles."*

But the voice of approbation was not the only voice that was heard in the land. Murmurs arose against the military leaders of the country, and it was savagely proclaimed that they were to blame for the long duration of a disastrous war. The end of these complaints was that Hindenburg and Ludendorff found themselves obliged to attend a meeting of a government examining committee to answer for their actions.

Ludendorff and Hindenburg stood together in this hour, as they had stood together on the eastern and western fronts. The committee tried to attach certain responsibilities to Ludendorff, and Hindenburg spoke. "General Ludendorff has always acted in full agreement with me. Who attacks him, therefore, also attacks me!" In face of these words, nothing could be done against the former First Quartermaster-General.

Both men had a tremendous reception in Berlin, and, when Hindenburg was led into the council chamber, every man in it rose to his feet, acting on an irresistible impulse, and thus they too offered their tribute to the man whom they were to "examine." The spleen and the hate faded after Hindenburg had said what he had to say. After this, there would not be found many men in Germany to raise their voices against him. His words had always the simplicity of a soldier, but they were strong with conviction and hope.

"In spite of everything," he said at this time, "I believe that Germany will rise again. . . . A people that has borne so monstrous a burden, until it has finally been torn to pieces, cannot sink for ever. . . . When work and order and national feeling return to us, we shall recover from the catastrophe. We must think of the men who died as heroes before the enemy and, in rebuilding the Fatherland, we must work as they did with equal faith and self-sacrifice—then all will be well. To my last hour, the re-birth of Germany shall be my only care, the subject of my fears and prayers."

So he returned to Hanover, cleared from any suspicion of guilt in connection with the war and its outcome. His welcome from the youth of the town was uproarious. The time at which his train was expected was announced in the lecture rooms, and these were promptly deserted; while the station was invaded by students who could not do enough to prove their devotion and admiration for their great fellow-citizen. They wished to "bring him home in triumph to his house." A short time later, these same enthusiastic spirits went as volunteers to help in suppressing the "red" outbreak in the Ruhr district, and, on their return, they marched past the field marshal's house to the stirring strains of the "Fridericus March."

Hindenburg's love for children and for the young led him often into their society. He played their games and treated their confidences with a sort of serious respect that endeared him to them all, but more especially to the grandchildren who were now growing up around him. Professor Theodor Lessing writes that he was once, temporarily, a master in a school at Hanover and it fell to his lot on some festive occasion to conduct a troop of boys to Hindenburg's house, where they were to sing *"Deutschland über alles."* The old man came out to speak to them, and he made a most profound impression upon Lessing, not so much by the words he spoke as by the conviction with which they were uttered.

"I should like to experience this moment again," writes

Lessing,[1] "with its mixture of sensations, union and equality with all children, the hearty laugh of overflowing spirits and the sacred humility; and above all, to feel once more my astonishment—for I had not held such a degree of childlikeness to be possible."

There was no indication that an old and experienced man was unbending to untutored youth—the impression given was simply that of a comrade talking to his contemporaries with complete understanding of their minds and hearts. And it is this deep accord with human beings of all ages that prevents the picture of Hindenburg from bearing a dangerous resemblance to that of a prig. There is something galling to erring humanity in the contemplation of a fellow human being who seems to be proof against all the voices that might lead him astray, whose first aim and object is always to devote himself to his immediate duty. The hard outline must be softened if it is to be regarded sympathetically; some warmth and color must be allowed to touch it.

Hindenburg saw in the children the hope of the future, and their importance, in his eyes, could not be exaggerated. They were to re-build Germany; they were to make up for the loss of the "glorious times of the German Empire," which had so suddenly and tragically disappeared. The Revolution had wounded him so deeply that he could not speak of it without betraying strong emotion, but the time was to come when he would be able to reconcile himself with the new Germany where there was no crowned head.

Hindenburg was now, however, to be tested by most poignant grief. His wife, after several operations, died on May

[1] "Hindenburg," by Theodor Lessing.

14, 1921, and the whole town followed her coffin to the grave. It was fortunate that his son was stationed just then at Hanover and was able, with his wife and children, to bring some comfort in this trouble, and to prevent Hindenburg's loneliness from being too extreme.

CHAPTER XIII

THE old soldier continued to pursue the even tenor of his way. He took a keen interest in German politics. His abhorrence of intrigue and diplomacy did not disappear, but rather increased in violence; for he saw with dismay how the many parties in Germany were serving to divide the country into factions.

Until 1919, Germany had been Nationalist in tendencies, but, when the Nationalists fell into discredit, the chief powers of the government fell into the hands of the Socialists, whose leader was Ebert, the first President, and a new order came into existence based on the Weimar Constitution of August, 1919. This was largely the work of Herr Hugo Preuss, Secretary of State for Home Affairs, who made the first draft, though this was afterwards changed to some extent. The new constitution came into force with its publication on the 13th of August, and it gave the political power to the members of the *Reichstag,* the elected representatives of the country. It lays down that the cabinet can stand only with the approval of the *Reichstag,* and that a withdrawal of that approval forces the cabinet to resign. In such a case the President is called upon to appoint a chancellor and to entrust him with the formation of a new cabinet, which has the approval of the *Reichstag.* According to this, new Germany is a parliamentary republic after the French example; but, so far as the election of the President is concerned, it differs entirely from the French system. Whereas the French President is elected by the deputies, the Weimar Constitution provides that the President of Germany must be elected, for a period of seven years, by the "universal, equal, direct and secret vote" of every citizen [1] who has reached the age of twenty. The same system applies to the election of the members of the *Reichstag;* it differs from the English system in that every vote is given to a party and not to a man, and that for every sixty thousand votes received by any one party, a candidate from that party's list becomes a member of the *Reichstag.* This constitution renders the President independent of the parliament, and enables him to keep himself outside of party divisions and influences.

From the inauguration of the Republic the Nationalists accused the Socialists of pandering to the late enemy, and of being so anxious to conciliate other nations that they threw dignity and honor to the winds. The country, as a whole, was torn by party dissensions and no single party had sufficient strength to carry out a definite policy. When the terrible inflation time came, many people thought it was directly due to the government's lack of policy in both foreign and home affairs. The inflation was most acutely felt by the middle classes, the supporters of the old régime, and they felt bitterly towards those who seemed careless of the old ideas [2] and inclined to a reconciliation with the rest of Europe rather than to an attempt to repair the losses of the war at home.

Roughly speaking, the population was divided into two

[1] Men and women.
[2] "Germany for the Germans."

FIELD-MARSHAL VON HINDENBURG AT THE TIME OF HIS NOMINATION
FOR THE PRESIDENCY

camps: one that worked for immediate results only and took no thought for the morrow; and one that would endure anything in the present, if by so doing a richer future might be bequeathed to the following generations. New parties were constantly coming into existence because of the discontent with which the struggles of the already established ones were regarded by the people. Germany, indeed, was again a house very much divided against itself. This state of affairs, however, was suddenly made very clear by the death of President Ebert.

Ebert had not been elected by the people in the manner established by the Weimar Constitution, but had been created President by the first National Assembly (*National Versammlung*) after the Revolution. At his death, no party felt strong enough to obtain a clear majority over all other parties for a future President. The result was a kind of amalgamation of the more important political groups. The candidate of the centre [1] parties was Dr. Marx; while the right-wing parties [2] supported Dr. Jarres. The preliminary elections showed that Jarres could scarcely hope for a victory over Marx and that the candidate of the Communists stood no chance whatever.

Seeing that Jarres stood in so precarious a position and had very little support in South Germany, the right-wing men took counsel together, and considered whether they had not better change their candidate. They sought a personality that would appeal to every one, and they thought of Hindenburg—Hindenburg, whose name still had a magic sound

---

[1] *Zentrum, Demokraten, Sozialdemokraten.*
[2] *Deutschnationale Volkspartei* and *Deutsche Volkspartei.*

in German ears, and whose army days had taken him into so many parts of Germany that he might be said to have a foothold in all the districts of the country. Hindenburg, the victor of Tannenberg and of the Masurian Lakes, and so nearly victor in France, was to be a leader now on a milder battlefield; for the war was to be waged with words instead of drums and with election slips instead of shells. It was the last battlefield of the old soldier, but the field was bloodless.

Henceforth retirement and peace, which he had so justly earned, were to be his no longer, for the fierce light that beats upon the thrones of kings shines also upon the less pretentious house of a President. Hindenburg knew well what he was giving up and realized fully the weight of what he was undertaking. But he considered no price too high to pay for the restoration of his country's fortunes, and he would spare no effort which he was able to make to contribute his personal share to the work. Perhaps, like Hiawatha, he had a vision of the country that was to arise in the future: and he was not the man to hold back because the task seemed too great. He could see only his duty, and knew that he must fulfil it.

CHAPTER XIV

WHEN Hindenburg was asked to accept the candidature for the presidency, he did not refuse: but he made it clear that he would not consent to be the tool of any political party. He would go his own way—the way which he regarded as the right one.

In accepting the candidature under any conditions whatever, it might appear superficially that Hindenburg was prostituting his instincts and his convictions for personal gain. He, the monarchist, the Prussian soldier, could not consent to be the President of a Republic without arousing the strongest possible comment both in Germany and abroad. Here again, however, as once before when he remained with the army and placed his services at Ebert's disposal, the observer must clearly see a subordination of self to the interests of the country. Was he, a monarchist, in accepting the seat of President, forswearing his oath to the Kaiser? No, for the Kaiser had left the country, and his action had absolved the soldiers from their oath. But so rigid a monarchist as Hindenburg could never consider himself released from the vow thus sworn—all he could do, to be true to it, was simply to remain in his retirement at Hanover until time should bear him and his honor to the grave. There can be no doubt that inclination spoke thus. Also he was old, so old that no one could have reproached him had he decided to act in accordance with his inclinations. He saw, however, that his country needed him, and the voice of the country was one to which so ardent a patriot could not close his ears. Germany was trying to rebuild her fortunes and recover from her losses, and she desired his help in this work. Duty called him from his house in Hanover, and he obeyed the call. And, in his famous Easter Bulletin of 1925, he explains the reasons which led him once more to take an active share in the future of his country. It reads:

To the German People:

   Germans of all races and provinces who have at heart the well-being of the Fatherland have offered me the highest post in the State. I obey this call, after long reflection, in homage to the Fatherland. My life is open before the whole world. I believe that even in difficult times, I have done my duty. If duty orders me now, without consideration of party, person, origin and profession, to act as President upon the basis of the constitution, I shall not fail. As a soldier I have always thought of the whole nation and not of parties. These are necessary in a state ruled by a parliament, but the head of the state must stand above them, and, independently of them, must rule for every subject. I have never lost my faith in the German people and in the support of God. But I am no longer young enough to believe in sudden changes. No war, no inner insurrection can serve to free our fettered and disunited nation. It needs long, quiet, peaceful work. It needs above everything to be delivered from those who have made a business of politics. No state can exist without order and without purity in its public life. The President is especially called upon to uphold the sacredness of justice. Just as the first President, even when he became the defender of the constitution, never denied his origin from the Social Democratic working classes, so no one shall ever be able to presume that I have given up my political convictions. Like Dr. Jarres, whom I highly esteem, at this time I do not consider the form of government of principal importance, but the spirit which pervades that form. I stretch out my hand to every German who thinks nationally, who protects the dignity of the

German name at home and abroad, and who desires freedom of worship and class understanding, and put to him the request: "Help me, too, to work for the resurrection of the Fatherland!"

Hindenburg thus accepted the candidature, but there were many voices raised in protest both in Germany and abroad. Some people, among them many who were devoted to Hindenburg, declared that the voting would go against him because of his age [1] and that those responsible for his re-entry upon the stage of active affairs would incur much reproach. Others stated that he had been made the dupe of party politics. Some declared that he would start a new war; and some that his election would add to the unpopularity of Germany abroad. But the dissentient voices failed to carry the day. The victor of Tannenberg had behind him the love and esteem of the great mass of the people of his country. He was a man of whom none dared say that he came to his high office otherwise than with clean hands; he was no mere party politician. His personality was superior to all such considerations as those of party; he was Hindenburg for the German people, and Hindenburg for the Nationalists, Socialists, and Social Democrats. He was equally trusted by all, and the result of the election was almost a foregone conclusion.

On April 26, he was elected President, with 14,655,766 votes, and with a majority of roughly 900,000 over his opponent, Dr. Marx. The telegraph wires got to work, and the news was soon spread all over the world. The effect of the announcement is well known. Some of the papers saw in the result of the election a step towards the restoration of the monarchy. They saw Hindenburg simply as a repre-

[1] He was seventy-seven.

sentative of the discredited German militarist class, and they thought that the hour of its restoration was approaching. It was not possible that Hindenburg the soldier would be content with anything else. He was too old, too set in tradition, to think of compromise. Little by little, however, the awakened distrust died down, and it was not long before the foreign papers were able to praise the bearing and policy of the new President.

Hindenburg said good-bye to Hanover and to his retirement, and on May 11, 1925, he made his triumphal entry into the capital. It was the third time he had taken part in a triumphal progress through Berlin—but this occasion was in great contrast to the first two. Once, when little more than a boy, after the war with Austria, he rode in the train of the King of Prussia on a September day in 1866. The second time was in June, 1871, behind the first Kaiser, on his return from France. Now, in 1925, himself the central figure, he entered Berlin, as the chief representative of a new order. Now, as then, the streets were hung with flags, and the houses were garlanded. Now, as then, dense crowds of people thronged the pavements and shouted their welcome —only the pageantry of monarchy was missing, and instead of a uniformed king a soberly clad President was the subject of the acclamations.

On May 12 Hindenburg entered the *Reichstag* in company with its President, Herr Löbe. The field marshal's entry was the signal for all those present to rise to their feet. He took up his position upon the flower-decked platform, under the black eagle on the wall. There was a silence, which was broken by the voice of Herr Löbe.

FIELD-MARSHAL VON HINDENBURG, THE NATIONALISTIC CANDIDATE FOR
THE GERMAN PRESIDENTIAL ELECTION

PRESIDENT VON HINDENBURG

HERR FELDMARSCHALL:

The German people, at the election of April 26, chose you to be the President, and you have been called upon to fill the highest, most honorable place in the German Republic. Article 42 of the Weimar Constitution ordains that you shall swear the Oath of the Constitution before the assembled representatives of the people. I have called the members of the *Reichstag* together to witness this solemn act, and I now hand you the form prescribed and ask you to swear this oath.

The President elect then made reply:

I swear by God, the Almighty and Omniscient, that I will devote my strength to the welfare of the German people, care for its prosperity, preserve it from harm, support the constitution and the laws of the country, conscientiously fulfil my duties, and maintain justice towards all men. So help me God.

The few serious words were spoken with deep sincerity, and they broke a silence so profound that it almost seemed as if the members of the *Reichstag* had ceased to breathe. The taking of the oath made Hindenburg the President of his country, and, after a speech of welcome delivered by Herr Löbe, he replied in clear, forceful tones:

HERR REICHSTAGSPRÄSIDENT:

Accept my most hearty thanks for the words of welcome you have just spoken in the name of the people's representatives, on my taking the oath according to the Constitution of August 11, 1919. *Reichstag* and President belong together, because they are both directly chosen by the people. Upon this basis alone rests their power. Both together incorporate the sovereignty of the people, which forms the ground of our political constitutional life. That is the deep meaning of the constitution to which just now I have most solemnly pledged myself. But, while the *Reichstag* is the place where differences of opinion [1] and of political conviction wrestle with one another, the President must serve all the working

[1] Hindenburg used the word *Weltanschauung* (outlook upon the world) for which there is no English translation.

and re-creative powers of the people, outside party interests. So, in this place, I wish once more expressly to state that I shall devote myself to the uniting of our people. This great task will certainly be made easier if, in this high house, party strife be concerned not with the advantage of one party or one profession, but with the question who can most faithfully and successfully serve our heavily tried people. I confidently hope that a noble rivalry in true fulfilment of duty will form a sure basis upon which, after the strife of intellect and opinions, we shall find common ground in the work that has been entrusted to us.

Rapturous applause greeted these brief sentences. Here was no glib politician who tried to dazzle one party or another, but rather a plain soldier who saw his duty before him and meant to do it. "I wish expressly to state that I shall devote myself to the uniting of our people, and to the rehabilitation of the Fatherland." No party should be able to claim the new President, for he would simply keep himself outside all party strife.

In the meantime, the crowds were waiting in the streets, impatient to greet their idol, for the personality of this stern martinet was haloed by the glamour of his achievements, and the people greeted not only their new President but their old field marshal. At a quarter past twelve the great doors of the *Reichstag* were opened, those doors which are so seldom used, and the new President appeared upon the grand staircase. A roar of applause greeted him and he was rapturously answered when he called for cheers for the German Fatherland. A perfect babel arose, however, when the chancellor (Dr. Luther) called out to the people: *"Unser Reichspräsident, Herr von Hindenburg, hoch! hoch! hoch!"*

CHAPTER XV

IT was indeed a heavy task for a man of seventy-seven years to undertake all the cares of state in so torn and distressed a country. Perhaps it was small wonder that at this time the newspapers told many stories of Hindenburg's "nervousness." So frequent were articles of this kind that an acquaintance of the President once asked him if they were true. "Oh," replied the great man, "I always whistle when I am nervous." "But," remarked a friend, who overheard the conversation, "I have never heard you whistle." "Well," said Hindenburg, "I haven't yet!"

He was, indeed, undismayed by the great work which lay before him, and he was perfectly clear as to the policy he intended to pursue. He would work to unite the country and to lay at least the groundwork for its rehabilitation in the eyes of the world.

After the war was over and the inflation had passed, every thinking man in Germany, no matter what his political views might be, realized the urgent necessity of rebuilding the physical health of the nation. No country could hope to rise from disaster if its population were shattered by ill-health, and above all if its children were not helped to recover from the effects of under-nourishment. In the days before the war, every man had to undergo his two years of military service and to submit himself, during that time, to the most rigid mental and physical discipline; and at the end of his service he was not allowed simply to fall back into ways of slackness, but had, each year, to attend camp where he was again marched and drilled into fitness, should he have allowed himself to slack.

The army existed no longer, and a great vehicle for the training of young men had therefore disappeared. Something had to be found to take its place, and that something was sport. The Germans have always been expert gymnasts and swimmers, but they never played games universally, as the English do, for instance. Football, swimming, cycling, tennis, rowing, riding and, where nothing else was possible, walking, were eagerly taken up in every province. The weekends found young and old people streaming to the nearest athletic grounds and rivers so as not to be left behind in the competition for physical health. So great was the enthusiasm that the organized *Sportgemeinde*,[1] a society that kept itself free from political considerations, had enrolled 7,000,-000 members. Ebert, the first President of the German Republic, had regarded the sport movement with great sympathy, and had always done what he could to further it, but its members received the news of Hindenburg's election with the most unrestrained rejoicing, for they realized that the new holder of the first place in the land had, in his youth, undergone the bodily discipline of the Cadet School, and they thought that he, more than any civilian, would be in a position to understand and sympathize with the aims and objects of the *Sportgemeinde*.

[1] Sport Association.

[164]

As a young man, Hindenburg had never played such games as tennis or cricket, nor had he taken part in track events; but he had always recognized the necessity of keeping fit. He walked, rode and shot, and he entertained, indeed, something like a passion for the last-mentioned sport. The day after the battle of Tannenberg he invited the chief forest-keeper of a neighboring estate to breakfast, and with him held a long and eager discussion about deer-stalking and hunting in general; and, as President of Germany, he did not cease to enjoy shooting. The members of the *Sportgemeinde* were right when they turned to Hindenburg for help and encouragement, for here, if nowhere else, existed a possibility of uniting all sorts and conditions of people into a compact whole.

Shortly after the war, there was some suggestion in foreign countries that Germany was secretly building up a new army "camouflaged" as a sport movement. Nothing could have been less true than this statement. Germany was simply trying then, as she does today, to replace in some measure the healthy physical training which her men had received in the days of compulsory service.

Hindenburg's sympathy with this sport movement and its aims was immediately aroused, and he received five officials of the *Sportgemeinde* shortly after he became President in order to hear what they had to say. He at once expressed his interest and promised to support the youth of the country in every way that lay in his power. On the next day he addressed the following letter to Dr. Lewald, the chairman of the State Committee for Physical Culture:

Berlin, June 19, 1925.

YOUR EXCELLENCY:

At yesterday's discussion with your Excellency and the other members of the State Committee, I was very much interested to hear of the work which is being done by the German State Committee for Physical Culture. I will emphatically support its efforts to promote the cause of physical training among the German people. Physical culture is a citizen's duty; it ensures the health of the people and demands action, "team spirit" and courage—characteristics which should form the basis of every healthy state.

For this reason I am glad to think that our youth is to be enjoined to work hard at gymnastics and sport, and that the whole population are to be encouraged, by means of building many sports grounds and practice fields, to use their bodies; it is with great pleasure that I follow the state competitions and games and I am also very glad that the State Committee for Physical Culture has undertaken that German youth shall be represented again at the international Olympic games, so that the world may be shown that the strength of the German people is inexhaustible.

I regard as specially praiseworthy the foundation of the school for physical culture, where organized bodily culture is taught, and I am glad to realize that the government and the state of Prussia have recently generously helped to complete the German school for physical culture and the German stadiums. At the same time, the authorities cannot bear the full·weight of financing so gigantic an undertaking, and I therefore hope that those sections of the population who are in a position to do so will further subscribe towards the building of the German "Sport Forum" and the other efforts of the State Committee for Physical Culture.

To give physical training is to serve the Fatherland!

I wish to express my thanks to the State Committee for its past activities and my best wishes for its future.

I remain, etc.

VON HINDENBURG

On October 18 of the same year the President laid the foundation stone of the Sport Forum, and, the ceremony finished, he addressed a few words to the spectators:

"German youth," he said, "to whom this building is dedi-
cated, be true, be united, be strong and hard!"

There was always something military in the way in which
he addressed those who distinguished themselves in the
realm of sport. Thus, when a victorious team of gymnasts,
lately returned from a brilliantly successful tour of America,
was introduced to him, he told its members that he hoped
all German gymnastic teams would always be found, as this
one had been, "at their posts."

Hindenburg, as an old officer, took an intensely personal
interest in riding. He attended equestrian exhibitions and
horse-shows in Berlin, and, whenever his travels took him
through districts which were renowned for horse-breeding,
he inspected farms and stables and showed his pleasure in
the work that was there being carried out. His interest in
racing was also great. *Hoppegarten* [1] saw him frequently,
and one of the annual Classic Events there is a race called
"the Hindenburg."

He also recognized the importance of swimming, and he
spoke on one occasion with anxiety about the number of
people who lost their lives each year by drowning. The
Society for Life-Saving, whose object was to teach every
swimmer how to save life, met with his most profound
approval.

So personal and so active was his interest in the sport
movement that he attended as many events and festivals in
connection with it as he possibly could. He founded many
prizes and gave his close attention to all details brought to
his attention. His trust in the healthy youth of the country
never faltered, nor did his hope that from it would spring

[1] Berlin racecourse.

the re-builders of the great nation; and this was the reason
for his strong support of the *Sportgemeinde.*

His conscience, however, did not allow him to overlook
the importance to youth of work. Upon his own writing-
table, as upon his father's before him, stood a little shield
bearing the words *"Ora et labora,"* and it might be said that
these three words were his watchwords throughout his long
life. Pray and work! Himself a rigid Protestant, he possessed nevertheless a wide tolerance towards all forms of
worship. When, in July, 1925, he received representatives
of Evangelical, Catholic and Jewish churches, he addressed
to them the following words:

Your united declaration that you will use the religious powers
of the German people whose representatives you are for the main-
tenance of the state and the re-building of our beloved Fatherland
has filled me with the deepest satisfaction. I see in it a valuable
guarantee for our home conditions, all the more because I am so
fully alive to the great function of the religious bodies in directing
the spiritual life of the nation. I take this opportunity once more to
assure you that, in my high office, I shall respect all beliefs and
all points of view with equal conscientiousness; and shall always
cherish the spiritual life of our people. If I may make a request, I
should like you to regard this reception of the representatives of
different beliefs by the representative of the German State as more
than merely perfunctory. As you, gentlemen, have come here to
express your common good wishes towards myself, so may also your
various churches and societies always strive to achieve that conciliation, that respect for one another, and that ground for common
work without which the future of Germany cannot be secured.

Thus, on every public occasion, Hindenburg always stressed
the need for co-operation among the different sections of the
people. He saw no salvation in anything but in union and
in working for a common ideal. The common ideal, how-

ever, was to be the rehabilitation of the country by means of a healthy home life, and not by means of an obsequious pandering to the rest of Europe. A restored, a revitalized nation should in the future receive her due from the rest of the world: a young, new generation should retrieve the lost battle—not indeed in a new war but in the re-birth of a mighty nation.

Even before he became President, Hindenburg stood in close relationship with many elementary and public schools and universities. Many honorary degrees were conferred upon him, and a number of schools throughout Germany bear his name. He exchanged many letters with the masters and boys of these schools, and to these he always appealed for team work, for enthusiasm in work and play and for a desire to help to raise the fallen fortunes of the country, to be encouraged amongst even the youngest. Georg Brandes once wrote [1] that when Germany fell away from the teaching of her greatest son, Goethe, she fell from her place of honor in the world—and Hindenburg realized that a profound respect for that past culture, whose brightest ornament was Goethe, should be inculcated in the growing generation. The war might have been lost, commercial prosperity might have disappeared and the monarchy have fallen—but this at least remained. The great culture of the past, the heritage of literature and music that belongs so intimately to every German, could never be taken away. And, with such an inheritance to support her, Germany should rise again, purified and revivified by the dark period through which she had passed.

[1] "Goethe" by Georg Brandes (the introduction).

On May 10, 1926, Hindenburg spoke at Weimar and emphasized the importance to Germany of her intellectual life.

There are two towns . . . which are especially dear to and honored by us and which, in all German eyes, are shrines: they are Wartburg, so rich in legend, the heart and centre of the first German poesy; and classic Weimar, which represents to us the supreme height of German poetry and intellectual development. And now, in these dark and heavy days which fate has allotted to us, many of us have gratefully realized how strong a power lies in our spiritual and cultural estates and how much comfort and confidence they can give us. Only the completest use of these inward powers can lead us back to health and worth; and we must all strive doubly hard in the present time to keep alive in our people the sacred fire of the ideal, that we may not lose a precious part of our existence and our nationality.

These are not the words of an ingrained "Diehard" militarist of the old school, but of a wise, kindly man who knows where to pay his tribute. They are words not unworthy to be spoken in the town where Goethe died.

CHAPTER XVI

ACCORDING to the Constitution of Weimar, the President of the German Republic enjoys also the supreme command over the army and navy, and to this post the greatest soldier in the country brought all the keenness of his martial spirit. To the young new army, Hindenburg became the great example, the possessor of all military virtues, and the symbol of past glories. He proved himself ever ready to come to the aid of any soldier with advice and help, and he placed himself upon a footing of comradeship with the republican army that endeared him to officers and men alike.

On May 12th, 1925, upon the very day when he swore the oath to the Constitution, he sent the following message to the soldiers and sailors of the Republic:

The trust of the German people has called me to the highest position in the state. According to the Constitution, I take over today the command of the army and navy, and I greet them with pride and pleasure. I have watched their development from Hanover, my place of retirement. This has steadily and truly followed the path along which alone the German people may hope to rise again: to achieve ability and success by means of stern discipline and devotion to the smallest details of duty. Its roots lie deep in the old sense of duty and sacrifice, but its dealings are for the present and the future, for the service of the people and the state, and it is faithful to the task that the Constitution has laid upon it. I trust to the German soldiers and sailors to help me to obtain peace and prosperity for the Fatherland.

Hindenburg wished that the little standing army of the Republic should preserve the spirit that had existed among

THE BIOGRAPHY OF

the pre-war regiments. These new young men were not to forget that it was for them to perpetuate the great tradition that had been handed down to them; they were to be worthy of that great host of their countrymen whose bones rested under alien soil, who had breathed their last in the service of the Fatherland. The army never forgot Hindenburg the field marshal in the personality of Hindenburg the President, and he seemed in a way to belong exclusively to them.

On April 7, 1926, the forces did him honor on the sixtieth anniversary of his entry into the Prussian army. Officers of the old army, soldiers' associations, the standing army, and even private citizens came to congratulate him on this occasion. A color company of the new army entered his house in the morning bearing the flags of those regiments with which he had served. He met them at his door, and for the whole day these standards were set up in the great reception room of the President's palace. Dr. Gessler [1] brought the congratulations of the forces to Hindenburg, who answered:

You will surely understand that I, an old soldier, surrounded as I am today with these honorable and famous symbols, under the shadow of which most of my life has been passed, remember with longing and pain the soldiers of our proud old army. That was a people's army, which not only served its purpose of protecting the Fatherland, but which represented a place of education for the whole nation, a university which taught fulfilment of duty and patriotism. What we have lost with its disappearance, we cannot judge at the present time. The new *Reichswehr,* whose representatives I see before me, has had to be built up upon other principles: it is small in strength, and instead of the duty of compulsory service, freedom to serve, or not, has been granted. But, as the new army is connected with the old traditions of our military

[1] Minister to the Forces.

[172]

PRESIDENT VON HINDENBURG CELEBRATES THE SIXTIETH ANNIVERSARY
OF HIS ENTRANCE INTO THE GERMAN ARMY

past, and as it has undertaken to preserve the high virtues of self-less devotion to duty, absolute love of the Fatherland, and sacrificial bravery, it too has become a stronghold to perpetuate among our people the soldierly characteristics of the old days. I am convinced that, filled with this spirit, the new army and navy will be true to their oath and will faithfully perform their duty; and that they will be led, in spite of the tumults of the present day, by no other feeling than that of love for the Fatherland and by the conviction that the future of the German people can best be served by quiet, unselfish work.

Hindenburg, though he built all his hopes upon the young and upon the future, still clung to the spirit of those traditions which he had so long ago been trained to honor. He could not feel towards the new order as he had felt towards the old, and the representatives of the new army, though conscious of his willingness to help them in their work, heard an undertone of passion in his voice when he spoke of the old army, which was not there when he spoke about the new, and in the closing words of his address he adjured them always to be worthy of the deeds of their fathers, as he confidently believed they would be. It is not the least of Hindenburg's achievements that he was able to adjust himself to the conditions of post-war Germany and to play a leading part upon the stage of affairs although his personal feelings lay so deeply rooted in the past. He was certainly completely convinced that the new soldiers could achieve no higher glory than the emulation of their father's virtues would bestow upon them.

Over and over again, Hindenburg gave expression to his love and respect for his old comrades. Towns and districts asked him to write a few words of introduction in the volumes containing their rolls of honor.

"That we should strive to emulate our dead comrades is the most graceful thanks we can give them," he wrote on one such occasion.

And again, with unconquerable pride: "Victory and defeat are in the hands of God—but we, ourselves, are kings and masters of our honor."

At the German Army and Navy Memorial, he sounded a note of hope with the words: "I have witnessed the heroic struggle of my Fatherland, but I do not believe and never shall believe that it was a death struggle."

On February 28, 1926, the country held its Day of Mourning in commemoration of the dead. On this solemn occasion, he wrote the following words:

The German people think today in silent sorrow of their brothers who gave their lives in defence of their homes in the greatest of all wars. They went to their deaths for us. At the graves of our fallen, who sacrificed themselves for us all, dissension must be stilled. Before us in our sorrow the holy sacrifice of those who fell in the war stands reprovingly—they died that Germany might live. The greatest strength of Germany has grown always from sorrow. While the flags are waving today at half-mast and while great crowds unite silently to join in worthy memorial services, the determination must take root in us to realize in truth the German saying:

> *Nimmer wird das Reich zerstört,*
> *Wenn Ihr einig seid und treu!* [1]

Hindenburg's lifelong love and devotion belonged to the old army, and it always gave him an especial pleasure to meet the veterans who had survived from the wars of 1866 and 1870. So deeply did he feel himself bound to the

---

[1] The state shall never be destroyed,
If you remain united and true.

soldiers, that he never failed to accompany to the grave the body of any dead officer whom he had known personally; and neither distance, inclement weather, nor any other hindrance was allowed to interfere with this observance, for each of these dead had helped to uphold the honor of his country.

The present-day military situation in Germany is so different from the pre-war that Hindenburg spoke very seriously to a foreign newspaper correspondent. "Germany," he said, "from my professional viewpoint, is not in a position to defend herself against even a small neighboring state, for even countries like Poland and Czecho-Slovakia have a far larger standing army than we, and are protected moreover by military alliances, so that in every case we should have to stand against a far larger opposing force."

CHAPTER XVII

Owing to the fact that the German President is elected by the votes of all the people in the country, it stands to reason that the man elected must have the support of the majority of workers of the great army of the employed. Were all these "little" people to vote solidly against any candidate for the position of President, his election would be rendered impossible. Hindenburg, whose personality rose high above class and party strife, was to the workers almost what he was to the soldiers, and they felt that one who held to the lofty ideals of co-operation and regeneration would help them, too, in the difficult times through which they had to pass. For, when unemployment is rife, when wages are low, and when employers have to fight to keep their heads above water, the workers are bound to suffer. And, when Hindenburg submitted himself as a candidate for the presidency, a considerable part of the *Arbeiterschaft* [1] voted for him, even supporting him against Dr. Marx, the candidate jointly named by the Central parties. Just as this large section of the community saw in Ebert a man who was one of themselves, a fact which they never forgot, and which he, himself, lost no opportunity of proclaiming, so they saw in Hindenburg the rescuer of East Prussia from the horrors of Russian invasion and the man who had, in the final moment of chaos, remained at his post in the service of the

[1] Labor group.

country. And, although he was essentially a soldier, he was very popular among the working people of genuinely pacifist post-war Germany.

When it became known that Hindenburg had accepted the candidature for the presidency, a section of the workers of the country displayed their faith in him by sending a deputation to his house in Hanover to thank him for his acceptance. The field marshal's reply was:

These kind words shall not echo in vain. I have always acted according to the principle: Faith for faith, trust for trust. We can advance socially only if all the labor units of the nation work honorably together. What I can do in this way, I shall do. I am a man who, with God's help, energetically carried out His will. It would be good, if we could now see national and social concepts brought into close communication with each other.

Hindenburg, in common with all simple and upright natures, was always able to find a basis of understanding with all sorts and conditions of men. He was alive to the national importance of German commerce, but he did not rely simply upon the commercial "kings" to achieve the necessary prosperity. No trade can flourish if it is served by disgruntled workers, and Hindenburg knew that the surest way to prevent discontent and murmuring was to ensure the best possible conditions for the laborers. Ruthless suppression of the discontented would have been the reply of a Bismarck to such murmurs; but Hindenburg showed quite another spirit in his dealings with them. He had only one object to achieve—and that was to be achieved by mutual understanding between all sections of society.

For post-war Germany, however, exactly this understanding was the most difficult thing to achieve. The old saying that love flies out by the window when poverty enters the door applies equally well to countries and to individuals. The colossal burden of the war debts made it a superhuman task to keep the state above water. Wages did not increase in proportion to the cost of living, and the laborers were told that they must give of their best without hope of reward for the sake of the country and the future. Employers were forced to retrench and to economize in every possible way. Liquidations were, and still are, frequent; long credits had to be given, and the government had to devote the whole of its abilities and powers to stabilizing the financial situation. It is not difficult to appreciate the fearful brink upon which the country trembles even to this day. There is fear in the country that, should another period of inflation come, Communism would follow it. It is scarcely too much to say that had Hindenburg not been elected President, the Communist movement would have spread to a far greater extent than it has done.

In order to pay her war debts, Germany is obliged to manufacture cheaply and to do an enormous export trade, and only by keeping every business and industry up to the highest pitch of efficiency can this be achieved. But the effort to make both ends meet has been a terrible one, and it has told most savagely upon the man with little capital and upon the workers.

Hindenburg felt deeply the need to lighten the conditions under which the laborers lived and worked. It was not very long before his name was signed below a number of acts dealing with social and industrial matters. In July, 1925, the accident insurance law was reformed and the health insurance law was redrafted. Further enactments dealing with old-age pensions and the limitation of child labor were followed in December by a law regarding the reduction of wage taxes. In 1926, laws were passed in connection with the mine workers, the housing question and the protection of older employees.

One of the most important social improvements introduced during the earlier part of Hindenburg's term of office was the establishment of the *Arbeitsgerichte*.[1] All disputes and difficulties between employers and employed are now submitted to a tribunal consisting of a professional judge, an employer and an employee. Hindenburg was especially interested in the establishment of these courts and in the improvement of the law dealing with insurance of workers against unemployment, which gave the workers of Germany an assurance that their claims were receiving due attention from the government. No employer in the country can displace a laborer without proper reasons. If a man obtains a post and behaves well, he may remain in it for the rest of his life, for any unjustified dismissal would at once be righted by the *Arbeitsgericht*.

But, although the laws which were enacted between 1925 and 1927 did much to bring Hindenburg's name into even greater honor among the people, there was a more magic, more personal side of the President which attached them to him. He let them feel that he could see no difference in worth between employer and employed so long as each did his duty. He, who had witnessed the political quarrels and differences of the day, had seen also the political quarrels

[1] Court of Labor.

and differences of other men who had long since passed into silence. It seemed that he realized the transitoriness of these things, and that he had found one genuine aim to strive for, one thing at least that would live through all time. To-morrow, other men would be striving for other political ends, but the work that Hindenburg had done would stand immovable as a rock because it was above the strife of the moment. Hindenburg really cared for the future prosperity of the people, and his request that the workers of the country should help him to achieve it did not fall on deaf ears. There were exceptions, of course, for there are always men to whom "long, quiet, peaceful work," especially when it is unaccompanied by any private reward, makes no appeal.

But, if Hindenburg demanded that the workers should help so far as lay in their power to leave a better world for the succeeding generations, he made equal demands upon employers. *"Ich dien"* was what he said of himself, and he asked no less from them. As a soldier he realized very completely that no one who has not learned to obey and to obey cheerfully has the right to give orders. He himself had obeyed, and, called to a position where he was in command, knew how to make his will effective.

Germany's trade and commerce were, and are, her life's blood. Hindenburg recognized the need of encouraging the men who were the directors of trade. They carried a very large share of public responsibility, and it was for them to devise means to improve Germany's financial status. And the fact that the whole strength of the country was needed to bring it back to some measure of life and health made it very difficult to give sufficient attention to less important questions. Unsparing and co-operative work was demanded, and by means of it disaster might be headed off and financial ruin prevented. The great personal example set by the President, whose clear blue eyes saw nothing but the immediate duty in hand, was such that it had real effect upon all who came into personal contact with him and upon many who did not. In a wild, insistent world where everyone tried to snatch what he could for himself, where everyone craved security and none had it, he was like a stronghold, and many people found courage to fight with a ruthless fate and learned, like him, to look forward to a brighter and easier future.

CHAPTER XVIII

ONE group of people in Germany voted almost to a man for Hindenburg; the agricultural class—land-owners and farmers, who had been seriously alarmed by the attitude of the Socialists towards property. From the disappearance of the monarchy and the reigning princes, it was not a very far cry to the seizure of the property of the big land-owner and its division into small farms and holdings. And, if large estates were split up and shared out, it did not seem impossible that smaller ones would soon share their fate. That all land should belong to the state and simply be farmed out by the government is a definite Socialist maxim, and, although land-owners whose estates were thus confiscated and divided were compensated in money, everyone knows that when a family have their roots deep in the soil, their farmhouse and the acres surrounding it mean everything to them. It is *their* ground, *their* property—and it would not be the same to them were it state property which they simply farmed during their lifetime. The agriculturists of Germany were conservative. If they did not actually desire the restoration of the monarchy, they at least desired that property should remain inviolable and that something, at least, of the old spirit should remain vested in the land.

The farmers complained that the government inspection of their farms and the wartime regulation under which they had had to sell their produce at fixed prices (with the exception only of what they needed for their own households and as seed for the next year's crops) had hit them so hard that they had scarcely been able to carry on. The measures taken towards equitable and fair distribution of foodstuffs unfortunately did nothing to help the farmer to increase his productiveness, or even to ensure that it remained at pre-war level; and the result was that many farms, at a time when every acre should have been tilled, produced fifty per cent less food than they had done before the war. When Hindenburg took over the supreme command of the armies, the agriculturalists turned to him for help and they found sympathy and strong support. Both Hindenburg and Ludendorff urged the necessity of increasing food production and not hampering it; but, by the time these two men stood at the head of affairs, the situation had become too serious to mend. Had the farmers been supported and encouraged to produce to their utmost capacity at the very beginning of the war, many people believe that, despite the blockade, Germany would not have suffered the bitter food distress of the years from 1916 through 1918.

Hindenburg, who was the descendant of a family of land-owners and soldiers, was, in addition, the man who had kept the country clear of the enemy, the man who had freed East Prussia, and who had, as well as he could, supported the farmers in the time of war. The land-owners felt that he would defend them somewhat against the inroads which the Socialist government seemed to be making on the rights and privileges which had so long belonged to the farmers.

It must always be remembered that Germany is a country consisting of many states, and, although they are united, each state guards jealously its own characteristics and its own borders. It might almost be said that, since the disappearance of the monarchy, there have been two opposing streams of opinion in the country, two conflicting ideas. The first was in favor of uniting and of centralizing all power in the central government, while the other saw in the preservation of the internal independence of the states the best means of furthering the ultimate ends of the German *Reich* and of keeping the citizens of each district contented and happy. Hindenburg was the man who stood in the centre of this conflict. He declared that historical considerations weighed with him and that he did not believe in a leveling which would have a deadening effect on all the states. Each must be allowed to preserve its characteristics, but he wished it to be clearly understood that, though each district might be left in peace to go its way quietly in matters of internal policy, this freedom must never be abused and must never be allowed to prejudice the unity of the whole *Reich*. A few days after Hindenburg became President, he made the following announcement:

To a large extent, we have to thank the independent life of the German states for the many-sided and fruitful intellectual development of our people. We should dry up the best sources of our culture if we were to lay violent hands on the independence of these countries. You may rest assured that I shall always make it my business to protect the just independence of the separate German states and to accede to their desires and their needs whenever I am able.

Small wonder, then, that the land-owners and farmers of these very states turned trustfully to the new President to support their claims. Hindenburg bound, so they thought, the stormy, uncertain present to the peaceful stability of the past; and they felt greatly relieved to see a man who represented the old order of things take their part when new laws came to be framed with regard to matters agricultural. The Socialists in the government seemed to be in favor of breaking up large properties, but Hindenburg proclaimed that property was inviolable; and so land-owners hoped that he would be able to exert an influence helpful to them. They saw in him a man who would represent the old order and help to reconcile it with the new; for the conservative land-owners and farmers were also ready to pull their weight and to help as best they could to restore Germany to her lost position in the world.

Hindenburg's personal interest in the land and its development was deep-rooted and sincere. He knew how great a measure of responsibility rested upon the shoulders of every man who owns a few acres of land, and he believed the agriculturists to be worthy of this responsibility, as is shown in some words he wrote in the *Deutsche Tageszeitung* on August 15, 1924:

I know that the German agriculturists will continue now, as previously, to put their whole strength at the service of the community. The heavy burdens which rest upon our sorely tested country, and especially upon the land-owner, must not and shall not be allowed to rob him of his courage. He must lead his countrymen by his unyielding good example, as he so often has in hard times in the past.

Per aspera ad astra!

v. HINDENBURG.

Hindenburg's personal connection with land-owners and farmers had always been very pleasant. In whatever state he had resided, he had always made friends among these people, had entertained them and had accepted their cordially offered hospitality. For men of the land, for the ploughmen, shepherds and foresters, he had the greatest possible admiration and respect, and many humble peasants throughout Germany could tell of how they had had long conversations about cattle, crops, timber and hunting, with a certain *"feiner Herr"* [1] who brought both knowledge and intelligence to bear upon the subject under discussion and who was always interested to hear of their own little troubles and successes. It cannot be too much emphasized that Hindenburg was always glad to speak to any man, from the highest to the lowest, and that he was as much at ease with cottagers as with his equals. He had that ease and simplicity of manner which an Englishman nearly always possesses, but which was a great exception in the case of a German brought up and educated as was Hindenburg. He was a great stickler for punctilio and etiquette in the army, and was renowned as an iron martinet who demanded the same high standards from those around him as he set for himself; but, when his uniform was laid aside and he retired into private life, he revealed a large and catholic attitude of mind which was little short of amazing in view of his training and heritage.

In particular Hindenburg made many friends among the green-uniformed foresters of Germany. These men, whose lives are spent in the open and whose business it is to care for and protect the deer and other game of the countryside, have also a very particular feeling for Hindenburg, who was

[1] Grand gentleman.

so keen a huntsman. The German forester thinks as much of preserving and protecting the animals under his care as of shooting them, and one of his maxims, "that an animal must be killed with the least possible pain and distress," might well be taken to heart by the huntsmen of other countries.

Hindenburg shot his first deer near Magdeburg after he became a commanding general. At that time, when he hunted, he made it his habit to stay with an old ranger and his sister, who lived in a wood. These days spent in the open and in such freedom and peace were greatly appreciated by the general who worked so hard. During the years of the war, whenever he could allow himself a few days' leave, these were mostly spent with old foresters in pursuit of deer or hare.

Some bad years came after the war. The winter of 1923 was so hard that nearly half of the wild animals died—all the care in the world did not avail to save them. The foresters therefore made an appeal to have shooting strictly limited in order to give time for recovery.

With the departure of the Kaiser, the sport of hunting suffered considerably. The new government had to concern itself with other matters than the preservation of game, and there was no one at the helm to pay any attention to the needs of the foresters. For the most part, too, the Socialists regarded hunting as a privilege of the wealthy, and it seemed more than likely that rude hands would soon be laid upon the cherished ideals and traditions of the woodsman. Then Hindenburg became President, and since he was a member of the old aristocracy and a great huntsman, upon whose coat-of-arms appeared the heads of a buffalo and of a hind standing under a tree, all rangers felt confident that their work would again be remembered in high places and that their traditions would not be heedlessly trampled under foot.

Hindenburg's election to the presidency, therefore, served more than anything else could have done to free the country people from their feelings of uncertainty and anxiety as to their future status. It must be realized also that Communism had gained a strong hold in Germany, and that when the land-owners saw the mines being drawn into the control of the Socialist government, and the land about to follow it into such control, they had developed a deep-seated fear regarding the future of their own personal possessions.

It has yet to be proved that state-owned land will be as carefully guarded and tilled as privately owned estates. It is certainly doubtful, for a human being is always more inclined to work for himself and his own heirs than he is for "the state." The state, at its very utmost, can only be a conception, perhaps an ideal. In the minds of most men, the state is only a vague thing which means much less to them than the two acres of ground which they possess. Hindenburg, who had passed from one state of affairs to another, stood between the two, trying to unite them in one cause and to keep what was best in both. For this reason the country people clung to him as to a sheet anchor. They were the ones who knew, as he did, the value of quiet work, of slow growth, and long maturing. They were wise in the lore of Nature, and the heritage of the fields was theirs; and they trusted that Hindenburg, who also loved the land, would help them through the trials of the moment.

CHAPTER XIX

HINDENBURG was able not only to bring all the sections of the community to a better understanding, but also to unite more closely all the widely different countries which are included in the German *Reich*. This he achieved not by means of political intrigue, but by the exercise of his own personal influence in each country. His visits to the various parts of Germany served always to increase the cordiality between himself and the population, and it is well known that nothing serves better to smooth away difficulties than the exercise of a strong personal influence. In this connection, Hindenburg deserves all the praise that can be bestowed upon him, because he was always able to see the best side of the differing peoples that compose Germany. Most Prussians, and especially Prussians of the military type, are unable to see outside the boundaries of their own country. The world, for them, consists of Prussia and the rest—and, in their eyes, the rest compares badly with Prussia.

Prussian discipline and organization made Germany what she was. The Prussian soldier was the backbone of the marvellous pre-war Germany. The Prussian officer was certainly the most efficient military man in the world. And the country where these men were born and bred was a country of fertility and well-tilled fields. Its watchword was efficiency in things both great and small. Indeed, were the definition of genius as "an infinite capacity for taking pains" to be regarded as tenable, then it would have to be conceded that about seventy-five per cent of all Prussians were geniuses. Moreover, Prussians did not "let themselves go" on occasions of rejoicing in the way that characterized southern Germany, where the more simple and ingenuous populations enjoyed their high days and holidays with an unrestraint that was vaguely distasteful to the Prussians. The sharper, clearer speech of the north was contrasted with the softer, slower tones of the south Germans, and the latter were characterized as "plump." To this day, there is some lack of real cordiality between north and south Germans, and it is therefore doubly remarkable that Hindenburg, both by heritage and training a Prussian, was always able to live happily in the south. He liked the Rhinelanders and the Bavarians, the men of Baden and the men of Swabia. In his memoirs, he bears testimony to the fact that he found much to like in the Poles—an almost incredible statement to be made by a Prussian.

Prussia, of course, feels that it has a very special claim upon Hindenburg, not only because he was born there, but because he had defeated the Russians at Tannenberg and at the Masurian Lakes, and driven the rude alien from the invaded territory. In the year 1924, before there had been any talk of Hindenburg's becoming President, he laid the foundation stone of the National Monument, and, after the ceremony, made a tour through East Prussia. On this occasion, the stiff population cast its reserve to the winds, and young and old greeted the field marshal with boisterous cheers and acclamations. Crowds lined the streets down which he had to drive, flags waved, houses were garlanded, and bands played in his honor. And all this happened in Prussia—where the people do not lightly show their feelings. In the following year, the East Prussians gave a huge majority vote in his favor at the elections for the presidency. East Prussia will never forget that Hindenburg and his volunteers balked the efforts of the Bolshevist army to invade the unfortunate province, and although a part of it is now separated from the *Reich* by Polish territory, it remains German to the core.

But, if Prussians had the special claim on Hindenburg that he was their countryman, the men of the Rhineland had also a very deep feeling for the President. These had watched the progress of the war in France with an anxious fear, lest the enemy should make his way into their fair country. It was not only the soldiers in the trenches who fought and died to protect the country at their backs; it was the energetic and able leadership of Hindenburg that made it possible to keep the enemy at bay. The field marshal had also lived in the Rhine country as chief of the General Staff of the 8th Army at Coblenz. At that time he had been attracted, in spite of himself, by the gaiety of the people, although he could not quite accustom himself to their light-hearted treatment of what seemed to him serious. In 1920, he wrote a few hard words about the mooted separation of the Rhine country from Prussia, which he described as "frivolity and gross ingratitude." When he wrote those words, his mind doubtless went back to the year 1918, when he came back from France with his armies. It was in 1920, when he visited Duisberg, that, with his eyes fixed upon the mighty river, he said to a friend, "No one knows what feelings move me at this moment, when I see the Rhine again for the first time since 1918."

Speaking later in the day to the crowds which had assembled to honor him, the President, he spoke words which went home to all who heard them.

Today, for the first time since the Great War, I have stood again on the shore of our German Rhine. Each of you will understand that I have been deeply moved. The Rhine is our river of fate. It belonged to us when we were united—we lost it so soon as we became disunited. Therefore, let the Rhine always be a warning to us to hold together!

Shortly after Hindenburg became President, the people of the Rhineland celebrated the completion of the thousandth year of their union with the German *Reich*. In all the beautiful villages and stately towns by the river, the people made holiday in their own happy, characteristic way. They drank the wine from their vineyards and sang their famous old songs. Hindenburg, who never let pass any opportunity to say a word in season, wrote to the population of the Rhine country.

I send the greetings of the other peoples of the German *Reich* to their brothers and sisters by the German Rhine, on the occasion of the thousand-year festival. The idea of celebrating the completion of the thousand years of union between the *Reich* and the Rhineland arose in the minds of the Rhineland people. In all these celebrations, the contemporary race must be conscious that they are the responsible representatives of a mighty past. The whole living power of labor and culture which blooms in the Rhineland today rests upon the achievements of ancestors over a period stretching back for more than a thousand years. During the whole of this time, the Rhineland, as a boundary district, has over and over again had to suffer the onslaught of historic wars. Thus a population has arisen, which, despite its complete devotion to the affairs of the mind and in spite of a healthy joyousness of disposition, has yet been able to develop a proper share of that true German seriousness and political strength which are necessary to combat the many trials of the present day. In difficult hours, the Rhineland held firmly and faithfully to its historic union with Prussia and to its ties with the great German *Reich*. The whole German people wish to thank the Rhinelanders for this endurance and this devotion to the main aims of the *Reich*. It is my un-shakable belief that if all Germans remain true to these virtues, the sacred hour of freedom will soon strike for the Rhineland. We shall none of us rest until this aim has been achieved. God, who has always helped us in the past in the hour of distress, will also help us now!

VON HINDENBURG

In 1920 he visited many Rhineland towns, including Essen, Bonn, Düsseldorf, Cologne, Rheydt and Krefeld. He found himself in close touch with the people, who gave him a wonderful welcome, especially in those areas which had recently been evacuated by troops of occupation. Hinden-burg appealed everywhere to the people to work in unity and harmony for the sake of the whole *Reich,* and reiterated his assurance that he would always respect and uphold the historical independence of the different districts, so long as they, in their turn, were willing to contribute their best will towards the re-establishment of the whole country and would uphold its honor and dignity in the eyes of the world.

In August, 1925, Hindenburg visited Munich, the capital of Bavaria, that country of proud and independent people who wished to keep their independence. Here, everyone regarded the centralizing and leveling ideas of the Socialists with dislike and distrust. The Bavarians, who saw in Hindenburg a member of the old order and felt that they could trust him to support their claims for independence, gave him a rapturous welcome.

Hindenburg was greeted in Munich with a speech made by Dr. Held, the *Ministerpräsident* of Bavaria, to which he made the following reply:

> I thank you, *Herr Ministerpräsident,* for the kind words of welcome which you have spoken in the name of the Bavarian *Staatsregierung,*[1] and for the good wishes you have expressed towards me and my policy. . . . I have said that I consider the independent life of the different countries important to the intellectual and social development of the state, and have therefore proclaimed that I shall give due heed to their especial wishes. Please consider my visit to Munich today as an expression of my great desire to stand in close relationship with the different countries and to develop a direct intercourse with their leading men, so that I may know their personal opinions. Intimate co-operation between the state and the countries is essential if we are to lead our country back to its former high position. I am glad to hear, from your words, that the desire for unity and the will to work for the common welfare are alive and strong in Bavaria. In the hope that we shall be able, as I believe we shall, to meet the future in close co-operation, and with the sincere hope that a happy Bavaria may live in a strong and united Germany, I thank you once more for your good wishes, which I heartily reciprocate.

In May, 1926, Hindenburg visited the northern city of Hamburg. Here, he made·a tour of the harbor and the river Elbe on board the steamer "Deutschland," and he expressed his great pleasure at being able to travel on this ship, which he regarded as so fine an example of German workmanship—"that workmanship which shall bring us back to honor." In the evening he was entertained at a great banquet in the hall of the *Rathaus,* and in reply to a speech

[1] Local government.

from Dr. Petersen, the Lord Mayor, he once more spoke out
with regard to his favorite policy.

I thank you from my heart for the friendly greeting you have
given me, and for the renewed honor which is being done me by the
senate of the free Hanse-town of Hamburg. I should like to thank
all those who gave me so pleasant a welcome in the streets
and in the harbor today; for I recognize, in these greetings
from so many different sections of the population, a confirmation
of what you, *Herr Bürgermeister,* have just said about Hamburg's
loyalty to the German state, and I accept this testimony as typical
of the feelings and desires of all Germans.

You were right to remind us that this spirit is no sudden appari-
tion of the last ten years, but that Hamburg and its sister Hanse-
towns have been illuminated throughout their history with this
idea of united Germany. The Hanseatic policy was always a German policy. Hamburg was always a bridge which bound our country with the world; it was the centre where all the different threads
of German commerce were gathered before they passed out into
the foreign world. So I have always appreciated during the years
of the war and the difficult post-war time, what it must have meant
to you to see the great commercial harbor of Hamburg, formerly
lively with the shipping of the whole world, lying empty and
deserted; to know the great, proud merchant service fleet delivered
up, except for a poor remainder, and to see all the wide foreign connection which bound Hamburg with the trade of the world, torn
asunder.

But the old Hanseatic spirit has shown itself again here. I am
able to recognize and admire today the tenacious will and the courage with which Hamburg started the work of rebuilding, and
which is so remarkable an example to the whole of Germany of
what German strength and German energy can achieve. As I
sailed round the harbor today I was able to see with satisfaction
that the old Hamburg has come to life again and is once more
approaching her earlier position as a centre of shipping and trade.
What has been achieved here in a few years—years of poverty and
need—represents German work and German achievement at its
highest, born of a firm belief in the German future and carried on

with fine responsibility towards the German people and their country.

This spirit, which unites the daring of seaman to the activity of an experienced salesman, is not only a Hanseatic characteristic—it is also characteristic of Hamburg. Upon it rests the history of your town, and it embodies that desire to remain independent to which you, *Herr Bürgermeister,* have just now especially referred.

I can understand that you are proud of this independent government of yours and that you see in it the deepest roots of your strength. In the future, too, Hamburg must fulfil the great task of being Germany's intermediary in world trade, and I believe, with you, that it will carry out this task in the best manner, if it be left the form of government which it has possessed for centuries. It must, however, be the aim of all of us, while exploiting to the utmost the different capabilities and talents of the various German races and districts, to unite our full strength to form a strong, united and self-contained state; only thus shall we be able to maintain ourselves in the world and make a lighter future for our people.

With this wish, I raise my glass to the well-being and prosperity of Hamburg and to the happy future of our great country. I drink, then, to the free Hanse-town, Hamburg, and to our whole nation!

So impressed was Hindenburg with his visit to Hamburg and with what he saw there that he wrote the following letter to the senate:

I shall always remember with the greatest pleasure my visit to Hamburg and the many wonderful impressions which it gave me. I was able to see the town and the harbor of Hamburg in its untiring activity, and I saw how Hamburg, inspired by a single idea, labors energetically to advance to its old place. I ask you to be convinced that my most eager good wishes will always accompany the people of Hamburg along the path they have chosen to follow. I feel I can scarcely sufficiently thank you and the senate for the festive reception, and the citizens for the signs of friendly welcome which they accorded me. I would ask you to give a special word of thanks for their exemplary bearing in the carrying

PRESIDENT VON HINDENBURG AND GENERAL DIRECTOR HEINEKEN OF
THE NORDDEUTSCHE LLOYD, PRONOUNCING A "HOCH"

out of very difficult duties, a bearing which won my special admiration.

Hindenburg made a point of visiting the capitals of all the German states and everywhere he expressed his desire that each should help in the work of co-operation and revitalizing, while he repeatedly promised that all the particular little needs and desires of the individual countries should be allowed proper scope. In October, 1926, he visited Brunswick and again appealed for co-operation. He said:

I willingly give you the assurance that I see in the preservation of the historically developed characteristics of the German countries and the independent life that is founded upon them, one of the strongest roots of German culture and national life. The life of our people can unfold richly and beautifully because it is fed by so many different streams. But this individual unfolding must not be allowed to lead to disunion; it must carry us strongly towards co-operation. Only thus can we attain the re-birth of our social, cultural and national position. For this reason I am especially pleased to hear from your own mouths that you will serve the "German State with the best of your powers."

So an old soldier tirelessly traveled and spoke in all the German states, and everywhere he went he made his influence felt. From the foregoing speeches, it will be seen that the iron martinet, the hater of politics and diplomacy, had forced himself to grapple with the most acute problem of the moment and that he had achieved something like a solution for the time being.

Practically every phase of the history of the German nation had revealed attempts to unite the different countries, to form them into one compact whole. The fact that, formerly, all these countries were ruled by kings and princes, each fiercely jealous of his honor and his powers, prevented these efforts from ever gaining a very complete success. Bismarck, a man of iron, was able to forge the unwieldy links into an apparently strong chain; but in the hour of need, the chain broke once more. With the disappearance of the monarchy and the reigning princes of the different states, a union might have been effected, but unfortunately the different countries were still divided by the varying political views and social aims that actuated their populations. There seemed to be no way of reaching a settlement, no way of reconciling the different factions. At the death of Ebert, as has already been shown, it seemed more than likely that Germany would be faced with an even darker period of disruption and discord. And what was there to stand between the nation and that black abyss? And who was there capable of directing and controlling the conflicting feelings and conflicting interests?

There was one old man found in the country; one old man who refused to yield to the burden of his years, to be broken by private sorrow, to be embittered by the total disappearance of all that mattered to him or to withhold the final service which he could render to his country. The winds of chance might blow coldly, storms might buffet, and disturbing new influences might be at work in the land. But it was German land, and he saw one way to save it, to secure for it a safer future. "Long, quiet, peaceful work" and co-operation were the things for which he asked. He stood up and demanded in no uncertain tones that each man, whether his lot were cast in high places or in low, should give what he could of good will and labor to the redemption of the wounded nation.

Nor was he content to stand at the head of affairs and give his orders and make his official appearances as they were prescribed. There are those in Germany today who characterize Hindenburg as "a man of straw," and who cannot see what this same "man of straw" has achieved.

In all the countries of the *Reich,* he made it a point to establish a personal bond and a personal connection with the people and their local rulers. He towered above the petty strifes of the moment; in place of a party slogan he gave them all a broader watchword, a wider, purer ideal, and he led them by the light of his own example.

Whether Hindenburg completely succeeded in his efforts to unite the country must still remain open to question. It is hardly possible to form even an adequate judgment of what exactly he has achieved. The point to be borne in mind is that he was able to establish a personal connection, in most cases a happy one, between himself and the various countries; so that at least that slender link might hold each of those countries attached, through himself, to the whole state of which he had been appointed the head.

It must not be forgotten that the long journeys and the speeches and the ceaseless burdens of state affairs rested upon the shoulders of a very old man, but it is more than likely that his span of years contributed very considerably towards the weight of influence he was able to exercise. If he, at his age, could work so untiringly at a gigantic task, it was surely not too much to expect people who were young and strong to help him to achieve the aim for which he was striving. He was a very old man, but the fire of youth had not been quenched in him; his hope for the future and his confidence that Germany would regain her lost place were the things that kept him young. Some of his contemporaries may permit themselves to call him "a man of straw," but it is likely that posterity will recognize his greatness.

CHAPTER XX

HINDENBURG was a soldier, but he possessed a far wider adaptability than most soldiers are able to acquire. He had been destined for a military career, and he himself had not been attracted to any other profession. Heredity, training, education and environment had strengthened his natural inclinations. Because he was so completely devoted to his calling, he rose to the very height of his profession. He cared for nothing else in the world. He read historical and military works and gave himself wholly to the development of his talents. A great patriot, he regarded the army as the very life of the country, its all in all; when the army ceased to exist, he must have felt almost as if Germany had ceased to exist. Robbed of that interest, he was able to give his attention to the future, but this forced him to study politics, and finally to enter them. The soldier was practically obliged to become a new man and to build up his hopes for the future with tools which he had never learned how to use.

Perhaps the disappearance of the army was no bad thing for the development of his powers. Had he still been able to devote his attention to military matters, he would scarcely have been able to think out that policy which is known as the *"Hindenburg Linie."* As has been seen, this was simply to unite the country within itself by means of a process of uniting all the people through conciliation. That he should have thought along lines of conciliation and pacification argues that he never had the iron ideas of Bismarck, despite his own statement in the *Aus meinem Leben,* when he tells us that a state run according to the maxims of Bismarck had always appealed to him as an ideal. Bismarck succeeded in uniting the different countries and making them into a compact whole. The German Empire was his dream, which he was able to make reality. The work which Bismarck did, however, lived only for a few years; it was not proof against the weapons of "outrageous fortune." The work which Hindenburg has done is not so spectacular. He established no empire and he did not stand as a controlling force at the head of a vast organization which he himself had created. His person was not surrounded by the pomp and ceremony of court life; he was simply a black-coated President—the representative of a republic.

His influence, however, in all states and among all grades of society was little short of extraordinary. His all-enduring patience enabled him to give interested attention even to dull matters of daily routine and to the mass of details which came under his notice. During the war, when all kinds of people wrote to him under the flimsiest pretext (and there were people who wrote to tell him that they had just drunk his health, or that they had named their new baby "Paul" in his honor!), he made no complaint. He and his secretaries separated the wheat from the chaff, and sometimes, in his rare moments of rest, he would reply to some of his overwhelming number of correspondents. When he became President of the German Republic, he made it a rule to deal personally with his correspondence. Appeals for help and advice reached him from all over the country. It would have been impossible for one man to reply to all these and to investigate the different appeals, but when it was within his power to help, the opportunity to do so was never allowed to slip away.

One of the most difficult of Hindenburg's tasks was to unite the two different streams of opinion in Germany with regard to foreign relationships. Nationally minded people were in favor of concentrating on home affairs and of giving every ounce of mental and physical power to the re-establishment of the different institutions of national life. Among these were many who regarded the terms of the Versailles Treaty as definitely unjust, for they could see that their children would still have to suffer and to pay for a war with which they had had nothing to do. Germans, however, are people who face facts—and the population as a whole determined to make the best of a bad job, with surprisingly little rancor and bitterness. They settled down to work and used what powers they possessed to improve the general circumstances of the country, and it is certain that their efforts to retrieve their unhappy past were observed with no little admiration by their former enemies. The British armies of occupation on the Rhine would be able to testify to the friendly attitude of the people. Everyone in Germany hated the presence of foreign soldiers in their country, and particularly because the occupying troops remained so long after the war was over; but they did not show discourtesy to the Englishmen on the shores of the Rhine. In a very short time, indeed, the population was on definitely friendly terms with the British soldiers. There was an astonishing absence of ill-feeling which did credit to both races, but the Germans who thought nationally were sorry that the occupation lasted so long, and objected especially to the Negro troops brought into their country by the French.

Opposed to this way of thinking was the attitude of those who wished to conciliate the French, the English and indeed the whole world by means of an undignified policy which cast all self-respect to the winds. It is, of course, no bad thing for any country to stand well with foreign powers, and friendly relations are good for trade and commerce; and, it was upon commerce that Germany founded her highest hopes for future prosperity. But, when friendship has to be bought at the pride of self-respect and honor, then it is too dearly bought. No nation in the world, and especially no nation which has lost a war, can hope to gain anything by a process of self-abasement. Many of the protagonists of the "Conciliate the foreigners" policy were Jews. The Jew in Germany had for centuries been down-trodden, ignored and insulted. The aristocrats of the old school openly showed their abhorrence of the race, and the middle and lower classes followed their lead. But the Jews went quietly about their business. Later, when birth and breeding ceased to count for anything, money could buy high places, and that forceful intelligence and skill for which the Jews have always been distinguished could serve to keep what their money had bought. These and many others, then, were the originators of the "conciliation" movement. They hoped that something might be gained from such a policy. And these "conciliators" had no sense of belonging to the nation; they had no idea of working for the common welfare of the country. They made a show of patriotism where there was something to be achieved by being patriotic, but they had no intention of helping anyone except themselves. The people, therefore, who thought along national lines were doubly bitter against the "conciliators" because their ranks contained so many persons who might on occasion feign patriotism but who never felt it.

The nationally minded acclaimed Hindenburg and his policy of understanding between states. They cordially welcomed his repeated requests to all classes to work for the rehabilitation of the country from within. Indeed, at one time, the Nationalists claimed Hindenburg as a member of their party on the grounds of this expression of opinion, but he denied their right to do so, because he would not consent to work with any one party against another. He eschewed all party politics both before and after he became President; though we are bound to acknowledge that he was out of sympathy with those who wished to conciliate the rest of the world. He wished to stand well abroad, and his dealings with the ambassadors of various powers evidenced this desire—although he never showed any tendency towards that servility recommended by certain politicians in Germany.

In June, 1925, Hindenburg received Mr. Schurman, the newly appointed ambassador from the United States, in order that he might present his credentials. Mr. Schurman stated that it was the desire of America to cultivate the friendliest relations with Germany, and that it gave him very great pleasure to follow the instructions given him by his government. He went on to say that although the world

was in a state of peace, yet fear and mistrust still interfered
with the enjoyment of its benefits. It was not the intention
of America to interfere in European questions, and so he
would refrain from expressing any opinion upon political
matters then under discussion. He would, however, say that
he considered that Germany's efforts to establish a better
understanding with her late opponents were likely to have
generally beneficial results. He finished with the word:

With deep admiration for what Germany has contributed to
civilization in the past, and with firm belief in the capacity of
the German people to overcome their present difficulties, I have the
honor, your Excellency, to present to you the best wishes of the
President and the government of the United States of America for
the well-being and prosperity of Germany.

In a few dignified words, Hindenburg thanked the
ambassador for his good wishes and also expressed the
desire that Germany and America might preserve their
friendly relationship. In conclusion he said:

Rest assured that I and the German government, especially in
view of the many tokens of friendship that Germany has received
from the United States in these recent difficult years, are actuated
by the same intentions as your government. We shall do all that
lies in our power to lighten the execution of the many duties im-
posed by your responsible office. Besides the extensive commercial
connections which bind Germany and the United States of America,
our countries have always been attached by strong intellectual ties.
I do not doubt that you—a former student in three German
universities, a professor of world renown, and for many years
president of famous Cornell University (which has already sent us
a most excellent American representative in the person of the former
ambassador, Dr. Andrew D. White)—understand thoroughly the
cultural and intellectual relationship between America and Germany.
Your Excellency's comment upon the unsatisfactory state of affairs

in Europe, and your sympathetic valuation of the new steps taken by the German government to try to establish a better understanding between the nations, are proofs that you have a cordial appreciation of the political needs of the German people and of their honorable intention of achieving a true and lasting peace. I take this opportunity to express my most hearty thanks for the good wishes of the President and the government of the United States of America, and I welcome you most heartily in the name of the German government.

It was also in the month of June, 1925, that Dr. Frank, the Austrian Ambassador, presented his credentials to the President of Germany. Dr. Frank stated that the unchecked energies of the German people had acted as a spur to the Austrians in the crises with which they also were faced, and gave them much reassurance with regard to the future. Hindenburg replied:

We look with brotherly eyes upon the friend and neighbor who, with unshakable courage and dogged effort, defies the difficulties with which she is confronted in the rebuilding of her house. The noble characteristics of mind and heart that have always distinguished the Austrians confirm us in our steady belief that the good wishes which I and the German people entertain for the future of Austria will certainly be fulfilled. The deeply rooted feeling of community which is enshrined in the hearts of all Germans on each side of the boundary forms an indestructible tie and a valuable possession which (as is my sincerest wish) must have its effect upon communal work in all spheres of life. Please be assured that you will receive unreserved support from me and from the German government in this common work. I welcome you most cordially, in the name of the German nation.

In Ocotber, 1926, Lord d'Abernon left Berlin after having held the office of British ambassador for a period of six years. Hindenburg saw his departure with great regret, for he had always done everything possible to further friendship between England and Germany. In a farewell speech, Hindenburg thanked him for the great services he had rendered, and appealed through him to England and the rest of the world for a better understanding to be founded among all European nations. His welcome of Sir Ronald Lindsay, who succeeded Lord d'Abernon, contained a similar note of dignified appeal.

Thus Hindenburg has personally done all he can to re-establish cordiality between his country and the Allies, and it cannot be said that his efforts were unsuccessful.

The ambassadors themselves did all they could to meet his efforts half way. In the presence of Hindenburg, no one could maintain that he acted as a militarist; he never revealed any of the teeth and claws that the foreign press predicted he would reveal, when it became known that he had been elected President. From the day when he took oath in the presence of the assembled *Reichstag,* the one-time field marshal showed only a desire to establish a solid and lasting peace. His conduct caused the murmurs and the fears to die away—for it proved conclusively that the man of war was also capable of being a man of peace.

An American paper expressed what very many other foreign papers stated more or less strongly, when it printed the following paragraph at the time when Hindenburg was elected to the presidency of the German Republic:

The German people cannot evade the responsibility for Hindenburg's triumph and its consequences for Germany and the world. They had the consequences clearly before them. . . . In the eyes of the world, this choice of Germany's turns back the hand of progress upon the dial of time. It is a declaration that the German spirit has not changed. . . . The alarm is ringing in France and Central

Europe, and its echo will be heard across the North Sea and the Channel.

But the personality of Hindenburg and his quiet way of going about his business stilled this "alarm" and silenced every voice that was raised against him in foreign lands. Certainly, all was not tumult and fury in every foreign country over this fateful election, for, as Senator Borah wrote in April, 1925:

> I do not believe that the result of the election should arouse great excitement. I do not doubt that national feeling and national spirit will be born again in Germany. If these, however, should be guided into the right path, they would act helpfully, and I feel that this will happen. . . . I think that other countries would do better to understand that the German nation has the right to choose the man it wishes and that, until the facts speak otherwise, no one has the right to doubt that the German people are acting upon correct principles and are following a proper policy.

The following paragraph appeared in the Swedish *Nation* in April, 1925:

> Hindenburg was the savior of his country. He accomplished the most brilliant military deed of the World War when he checked the advance of the Russian steamroller and thereby freed the lands of the Baltic Sea from the yoke of Asia. That was a victory for European and world culture. But, in addition to this, he achieved in November, 1918, the great deed that Germany will never forget. When the fortunes of war forsook the German arms, when the flags had to be furled and the Kaiser went to Holland, he led the army home. Only his authority was strong enough for this deed; and in achieving it he spared the country much misery. Deeds like this are never forgotten by a people. It is one of the things that make it apparent why the people have made a choice in which the politically clever of this world detect political immaturity. The choice of the German people is perhaps not clever, because it can cause mistrust among their foreign opponents. But it is to be hoped

that these countries, which fought for democracy, will permit even a defeated country to choose as its head the man whom it wishes to appoint.

Another Swedish paper, however, the *Social Democrat*, took a decidedly different view:

The election of Hindenburg is the conquest of the German government by Nationalism and Militarism. It brings an incalculable element of unrest into European politics.

In Switzerland, the paper *La Suisse* commented more fitly upon the election of Hindenburg:

Curious and wonderful fate of a soldier, who, without wishing it, has united in his person all the hopes and all the good faith of a whole country! Of such a man one may believe what one will; but a chief who, without the exercise of manœuvre or tricks, but simply by the power of his patriotism, alone represents victory in a defeated country, deserves that even a former enemy should trust him, or at least should wait to see what he will do.

After Hindenburg had been President a few months, the *Daily News* [1] wrote that events had not justified the fears which his selection had naturally caused in England, and that Englishmen must accord him all the admiration which he had undoubtedly earned. This paper further praised the skill, moderation and dignified bearing he had shown ever since he had been appointed President.

On the 1st of January, 1926, the President's annual reception to the foreign ambassadors gave the other countries an opportunity to express their good will towards Hindenburg. This yearly reception is a stately affair and is attended by great ceremony. At mid-day the procession of ambassadorial cars rolls up to the principal entrance of the President's pal-

[1] November 2, 1925.

ace, and the uniformed representatives of the foreign countries make their way to the magnificent reception hall, where the President, assisted by his chancellor and foreign minister, receives them. One by one, in order of rank, these foreigners in their colored uniforms approach Hindenburg, who, by contrast, appears in the plain black and white of evening dress, relieved only by a few orders. On these occasions he wears the ribbon and star of the Order of the Black Eagle, the order Pour le Mérite and the Star of the Iron Cross—that "Blücherkreuz" which nobody but Blücher and Hindenburg has ever worn, and which no one else will ever wear.

In 1926, the dean of the diplomatic corps, the Apostolic Nuncio, expressed in French the good wishes of the collective nations. Dressed in his magnificent vestments, and wearing the jeweled mitre of his office, he yet could not dwarf the dignity of the plainly clad President, whose giant stature certainly needed no outward pomp to make it impressive. The Nuncio expressed the sincere hope that the efforts to obtain good feeling between all nations might be crowned with success, and complimented Hindenburg upon his conduct of affairs of state and upon the personal influence he had been able to exercise upon his countrymen.

"The diplomatic corps, whose voice I once more have the honor to be," he said, "brings its warmest good wishes for the New Year to the German people, who under your wise leadership are working in the most admirable way to achieve their peaceful rehabilitation; and we pray that God in His eternal love and inexhaustible goodness may, through His providence, bring these wishes to fulfillment."

Hindenburg's reply echoed this hope.

You spoke of the important happenings which have taken place upon the political stage during this past year, during the first months of my taking office. I hope, with you, that the wishes of all people, and especially the expectations of the still deeply depressed German population, will not be disappointed; with you, I hope in God's name that the seeds sown in an honest endeavor to reach an understanding will soon spring up into a true and full peace. The German people, whose hearts are deeply impregnated with the living truth that justice, morality and freedom are the only foundation stones upon which the mutual understanding of all people can be built and developed, will work on unsparingly for the peaceful rebuilding of its own national life according to the requirements and needs of peace. This alone can advance and raise the culture and commerce of the world. May the New Year into which we have just passed see our common wishes for a better understanding among the peoples brought to a living reality!

In his dealings with foreign powers or their representatives, Hindenburg always insisted upon Germany's right to perfect freedom in the conduct of her home affairs and the need of this freedom for the peaceful development not only of the German peoples but of the whole world. He always upheld the dignity of the German name, and pointed out the debt which the world owes to Germany in many intellectual spheres. His own dignity and simplicity and his manner of going straight to the point, rather than beating about the bush, were qualities which impressed all the foreign ambassadors. These men, well versed in the art of diplomacy—in knowing how to use language to conceal their thoughts—acknowledged that Hindenburg, through his more forthright and simple method, could accomplish as much as they in establishing good faith and understanding. There was never anything spectacular in the work which Hindenburg did as President, but he has been able partly to attain

PRESIDENT VON HINDENBURG RETURNING HOME FROM A WALK
IN HANOVER AT THE TIME OF HIS ELECTION

what was always his object. "Germany must and shall recapture her place of honor in the world"—that was what he had said, and that was the sum total of what he desired, the only thing that he cared about. And little by little, the whole world has been forced to acknowledge his achievement. Hindenburg, in changing from the dress of a soldier to the dress of a statesman, was fully able to make those qualities which had raised him to the head of the army serve him also in the carrying out of his duties as statesman and the representative of a great nation.

Hindenburg's greatness was not only to be seen in his actions, not only to be heard in what he said—it was also in the essence of his own character and of his private thoughts. His personality counted for more than his deeds or his words.

CHAPTER XXI

HINDENBURG sympathized deeply with those of his countrymen who lived in the occupied areas, and year after year, with great admiration, he watched their conduct; in the most trying circumstances, they behaved with praiseworthy moderation and dignity. The President therefore welcomed the opportunity in March, 1926, to visit the recently freed district of the Rhine. In Cologne, he attended a celebration in the great *Messehalle,* where a huge concourse of people listened eagerly to his address, which was as follows:

Every German heart felt bitter because the ancient German country on the Rhine, that cradle of German history and German personality, lay spiritually and physically separated from us, in the hands of foreign occupants. To all of us, the Rhine is the symbol of our great past, of our eventful history. In the land through which it flows, we see on all sides reminders of the development of our people; here, the German Kaisers were elected and crowned; here, the first German masters of poetry, art and architecture lived and worked; here, the first feelings of free citizenship unfolded out of the mists of time and gained force and saliency. This ground, so rich in beauty and cultivation, has also seen many wars; no other river district has been fought over so often as the Rhineland, and more than once these battles about the Rhine have influenced the development of our nation.

Throughout our history, the Rhine has been the river of our fate; it has often been a bright symbol of German strength and greatness, but it has also often been a dark picture of German suffering, especially when our old arch-failing—disunion—has paralyzed our strength. For this reason every German, from no matter what race he may spring, feels himself closely attached to the Rhine, and what you have suffered here in the last few years we have all felt as a national calamity; we have all suffered with you and sympathized with you from the bottom of our souls. We, the elected representatives of the nation, of Prussia and other German states, the citizens of the town of Cologne and her guests from the nation, have come here to celebrate together the fact that a part of the Rhineland has at last won back its freedom.

Yet other German suffering in the immediate past makes its voice heard. Painfully distressed, we must think of our brothers, in our otherwise proudly united country, who must still bear the burden of foreign occupation; with true and grateful hearts we send them our greetings in the hope that we shall soon be reunited in freedom. In this hour we all think with warm hearts and inextinguishable gratitude of those who, in the heavy troubles of the past years, gave up their lives and their freedom, and either gave up, or at least hazarded their homes, that they might be true to the country and to its honor. It will also never be forgotten that the Rhineland, in the hours of its own most bitter despair, continually asked the government not to make any political decisions with special view to the needs of the occupied territory, but always to take into consideration the combined interests of the whole country and to make decisions in accordance with the requirements of the whole German future.

All these sacrifices have not been made in vain; they have served to show the world in general that the people on the Rhine firmly and unyieldingly adhere to their nationality, they have steeled and hardened the patriotism of the whole Rhineland in the fire of trouble and they have demanded and strengthened, by their exemplary determination in war and danger, that unity of which we all stand in such need today. Through the difficult experiences of the past years, the weaponless fight that our men and women in the Ruhr and the Rhine have had to wage for their nationality, for their rights and for their freedom, has produced the deepest conviction that Germany is not by any means completely destroyed, that we are not on the way to ruin. We, like you who have fought this battle so bravely, shall all develop this trust in the future of Germany which, peacefully and strongly, shall reunite the land on the Rhine with the rest of Germany. And further, let us hope that the German people will also pass through the internal strife and trouble of the present to a complete unity and a strong sense of nationality. This must be achieved by means of a new spirit of brotherly understanding. That we may all be able to contribute something towards this must be our inward wish as we cry: May Germany, our dear country, live! Hurrah! Hurrah! Hurrah!

The last words of the President were drowned in the deafening cheers of the crowd. Hindenburg stood upon the platform and looked down upon them with a little, half-pathetic smile. He, too, rejoiced to see a part of his beloved Rhineland freed from the occupation—but he was now too old to feel that wild enthusiasm which he saw demonstrated before him. His eyes lingered upon the ranks of the students, and he searched those young faces for signs of the spirit which had animated their fathers and grandfathers. In these boys he placed his hopes for the future of the country; these who, in the full possession of their young powers, could still give so large a measure of their respect and their affection to an old man like himself. For, as the great man stood there in the *Messehalle,* he must have known that the cheers which the students gave were as much in his honor as in honor of the occasion which they were there to celebrate.

In the evening, Hindenburg stood on the balcony of the *Rathaus* to watch a torchlight procession of the different guilds and societies of Cologne and of the student corporations. For more than an hour, the torch-bearers passed in a long procession before the President, while he saluted the flags as they were borne down the streets. He again spoke to the crowds and appealed for unity and understanding, and was answered by the wild cheers of the people. Finally, the crowd took up the noble song, *"Deutschland über alles,"* and a great wave of harmony arose under the stars. Men and women joined together to sing that stately tune, and there were tears of profound emotion in many eyes as the last notes died away in the chill darkness of early spring.

As the several zones of the Rhine were successively evacuated, Hindenburg sent many messages to the inhabitants of the freed areas. All these speak constantly of reunion and of future hopes. None strikes any note of vindictiveness against the foreign soldiers; none contains a single word that could be offensive to the allied countries, but each reveals the depth of sorrow which Hindenburg suffered through the knowledge that Germany was not free, and each expresses his admiration for the conduct of the population in the occupied districts.

Hindenburg's sense of fitness was most remarkable, when it is remembered that he had had no training other than a military one, and when it is taken into account that he could not feel really at home in the realm of politics. He rose almost to superhuman greatness when he put the past resolutely behind him and gave his whole strength and the remaining years of his life to the services of a republican state. He had not been "nurtured in democracy," and, in order to help his country he had to discount his heredity, his traditions and training, and rise above all his own personal feelings. This he succeeded in doing and he never referred, on any public occasion, to the gods he had been brought up to worship.

To the young, new, democratic Germany, he spoke often

of the great name they had inherited. They must strive, he said, to be worthy of the great traditions of the past, and he was sure that they would pass through present darkness into a future that would be bright.

In the history of his country, Hindenburg will stand always as the last supporter of the old traditions and the first introducer of a note of hope into the surrounding chaos of the transition stage. How much the words he had to say counted among the students is evidenced by the fact that those who were studying in the western universities sent him a message of good will in which they declared that they wished to "show themselves as Germanic heirs who were worthy of their fathers." That they should be worthy of their fathers was all that Hindenburg had to ask of them, for he could imagine nothing better.

And, if the young were going to prove themselves true heirs of the men who had died to keep the foot of the stranger out of Germany; and if the peoples in the freed districts were going to emerge from the trials of the occupation with their feelings of patriotism heightened—then, indeed, he felt he was justified in looking with optimism towards the future, however dismal, however trying the present might be. If he did not live to see the day when Germany was absolutely free, he still would have done more than his share to fit the country for that freedom when it came.

CHAPTER XXII

MANY years before fate had called Hindenburg to the Presidency, he had worked for a period in the War Ministry. He had brought to his work there those immense powers of concentration and that untiring devotion to the task in hand, however distasteful that task might be, which had characterized him through every phase of his career. He wrote in his memoirs that this was a time upon which he could not look back with any degree of pleasure, though he recognized its importance to his military career. One thing, however, that he noticed during that time was the unflagging zeal of the minor clerks and their immediate superiors. He saw how quietly they went about their appointed business, year in and year out, and how uncomplainingly and conscientiously they fulfilled their duties, which to his soldier's mind seemed to be so uninspiring and uninteresting. He never forgot these pale-faced men in their plain, dark clothes, and how they succeeded in keeping the wheels of the office well oiled and smoothly running; and, upon his appointment to the Presidency, he had an opportunity of expressing his appreciation of the work done by the civil servants generally and of acknowledging their importance to the state.

Shortly after he had taken office, he received certain high officials of the civil service and, on this occasion, he spoke in generous praise of their work and its importance.

"I am fully aware," he said, "that the civil servants of Germany, by their unselfish and devoted work, have contributed in no small measure to the fact that, in the difficult years after the Revolution, the order of the State and the unity of the *Reich* remained safe. I also know how much you, gentlemen, have served the country and the German people by your untiring work, and I am convinced that, in the future, you will also lead the way for all the officials of the civil service, with the example of your most dutiful work. Today, it gives me a very keen pleasure to express my thanks and my admiration to you, as representatives of the civil service, as well as personally."

These were people of whom Hindenburg could very well express a sincere admiration. They were exponents of that "long, quiet, peaceful work" of which he thought so highly. Duty was their guiding star, as it had always been his own, and it was theirs to plod year after year through all the weary routine work which is necessary to the proper running of a State. They sat in their offices with their sheaves of documents and papers, and preserved order, and supplied information when it was required—and no one ever gave their work a thought; they received but small credit and recognition for the services they rendered.

When Hindenburg visited Düsseldorf in September, 1925, just after the first zone had been evacuated by the Allies, he took the opportunity once more to say words of recognition and encouragement to the civil servants who had carried out their work in the occupied areas of the country.

I feel it my duty, in the name of the state, to express to you and all other officials of the country the sincerest admiration for the gallant bearing which the civil servants of all grades have shown in the difficult years behind us, and to thank them for the faithful fulfilment of their duties and for the great sacrifices and heavy sufferings which they have borne for the sake of the country. In the difficulties of these times, the civil servants have shown themselves to be fully equal to their tasks, and have been a support to the people by putting their own welfare last; and, above all, they have set the country an example of courageous steadiness and unconditional devotion. In the honorable history of the German civil service, the unerring devotion to duty and the brave bearing of the officials in the Rhineland and Westphalia will form an especially famous page.

So it was that Hindenburg, with an eye that missed no detail, brought the work of the humbler officials to the light of day and found it good. It was through people like these that he sought personally to approach the various states of Germany and to form closer ties between them and the government at Berlin. For it was very essential that the lesser officials of the states should be in harmony with the government, because discord here might retard the progress of that "national" feeling which he so anxiously strove to encourage throughout the country. There is an old saying that tells how "for want of a nail" a horse's shoe was lost, and how the loss of the shoe led to the loss of a battle, and this ultimately to the loss of the cause. Hindenburg knew exactly the importance of every detail in the affairs of state, and he compelled others, through the pains he himself took in details, to follow his example. Germany, during the time after the Revolution, had a skin as senstive as that of the fairy-tale princess who was bruised by a pea which had twenty mattresses piled on top of it. The smallest discomfort, whether real or imagined, had to be avoided if possible, and it was urgently necessary to preserve good feeling everywhere.

The government, as has already been shown, had to devote the best of its powers and thought to conserving the financial situation and strengthening the prestige of the new Germany among foreign powers. It may be said that upon Hindenburg fell practically the whole weight of the work involved in reconciling and healing the different peoples within the country. It fell to his share to awaken in the discouraged and war-broken population a feeling of national pride. He, alone, tried to encourage the small, local authorities and officials to carry out their work with enthusiasm and for the sake of the German Republic. He made these men feel that their long years of patient work were not forgotten or despised; he made them realize just how responsible their posts were and how much depended upon them. This help and encouragement, which was always so utterly sincere, did more to awaken German national pride than anything else could have done. If a man is told by a highly superior official that he is of real importance and that his work is vital to the state, he will certainly be only too glad to agree. And, once the feeling of importance is established in the man, he will also take an added interest in his work and will be more efficient and happy. If the small, local authorities are efficient and happy, there will certainly be a more cordial relationship between them and the government than would otherwise be the case. So, Hindenburg's maxim that loyalty was due just as much from the officer towards the soldier as from the soldier towards the officer, and that both owed loyalty to the state, worked very beneficially in the ranks of the civil servants, for they enjoyed their moment of public approbation after the years during which they had worked and had no other reward than indifference towards their achievements. One of Hindenburg's greatest personal accomplishments was that he could make the veriest ploughboy feel the importance of his task and of himself to his country. Truly, Hindenburg the President had traveled a long way from Hindenburg the soldier.

The men, also, who were responsible for the administration of justice in the law courts found in Hindenburg a supporter who sternly upheld the independence of the courts of justice as being above all party questions. Justice, to him, was a sacred matter, with which no other considerations could be allowed to interfere. The poor man must have equal justice with the rich; the communist was to be as impartially treated as the conservative. In his *Easter Bulletin*, before the election to the presidency, Hindenburg made special reference to this, when he wrote that it was the duty of the President to uphold the "sacredness" of justice.

On March 2, 1926, he visited the law court at Leipzig, which is the highest court of justice in Germany. He wished to express his respect for this august court, the president of which received and welcomed him with a speech. Hindenburg made the following reply:

It gives me the greatest possible pleasure to visit the highest German law court. You are quite correct in interpreting this visit as a proof of the importance with which I regard the administration of justice. Justice is the basis and the soul of the state; and the higher the tide of political and social dissension arises, the more fundamental is the necessity of impartial justice, which, untouched by the passion of these battles, protects and upholds Right and Law

without favor or fear. For this reason, in our time, which is so
filled with political differences, it is more than ever essential to
preserve high justice and absolutely to prevent all attempts upon
its independence. Upon you, gentlemen, rests not only the task of
securing the single-minded reading of the German laws, and of
seeing that these are properly developed according to the needs
of the present day, but you have also to be leaders and examples
to all the German courts of justice in their effort to reach the highest protection. The history of this High Court [1] is sufficient proof
that it is able to do this; for the last half-century it has been
closely connected with the rise and development of the country.
Other great tasks are also laid upon you; commercial and social
problems continue to confront the courts of justice, and the law
is stretching new bridges beyond the boundaries of the country to
unite the people. Today, the hope that I have to express to you,
and through you to the collective courts of justice of the whole of
Germany, is that the work of your high and responsible office may
also continue to secure the well-being of our people; and I greet
you most cordially in the name of all those whom you serve.

Justice was, to Hindenburg, a matter of the utmost importance, and his respect for it was shown throughout the whole
of his military career—and most strikingly at the period
when he had to command Polish troops. Other officers of
the Prussian school had no good to say of these people, who
were often thievish and dirty, who had no sense of Prussian
discipline and usually but little knowledge of the German
tongue. They often suffered injustice and were the victims
of unfair treatment by both non-commissioned and commis-
sioned officers. Hindenburg, in his memoirs, certainly refers
to the regrettable frequency of petty thefts and other small
crimes among the Polish troops, but he also finds excuses
for them and further states that he found the Poles both

[1] The *Reichsgericht*.

willing and industrious. It may safely be said that very few other Prussian officers would have been found to endorse his views on the subject of the Poles, and that he was able to evolve such opinions was owing simply to his rigid sense of justice. He did not see results only—he looked also for causes, and, strict though he might be, he made allowances for circumstances.

When Hindenburg visited Leipzig, he also attended the great exhibition of German work and trade, and in the *Rathaus* he addressed a large gathering on the subject of what he had seen.

I can assure you that it has made a good impression upon me, here, at the foot of the War Memorial (that symbol of the great German past), to see in the great hall a kind of review of German work and German enterprise, in which not only a sign of an industrious and rising present may be seen, but also a hope for a new German commercial success in the future. The *Messe* of Leipzig, with its enormous organization and scope, has always given our people a comprehensive survey of the high quality of our work and of the technical abilities of our population. The Spring Exhibition of this year has struck a new note in that it gives special proof of the technical advances of German production, new methods of manufacture and new tools and materials; and these should give our impoverished commerce a greater scope in the use of its powers and should provide for successful results. We accompany the activities of these commercial pioneers on their way with great expectations and good wishes. Just as in previous centuries, even in the worst times of war and trouble, we never allowed the work of the *Messe* of Leipzig to be interrupted, so, today, shortly after the great World War, this *Messe* is once more a symbol of continuous extension and technical development of our trade and commerce, and is an important means of furthering all the interests of commercial dealing. This year, the *Messe* has especially undertaken to give German trade a spur and an encouragement. The trade crisis lies heavily upon all sections of our people; millions of industrious people have been condemned to unemployment and misery; and the German employers are fighting with the most adverse conditions. The *Messe* of Leipzig should and does prove its value in just these situations: it gives a chance to strengthen mutual trust among the people of trade circles and gives new life to the attempts to establish new business connections at home and abroad; and it shows the world that the strength and will of German commerce have remained unbroken.

So Hindenburg went from the south of Germany to the north, from the east to the west, and everywhere he spoke words of hope and encouragement; and, although he always dwelt upon the future success which he so confidently believed must follow present efforts, he did not ignore the manifold difficulties with which practically every group of people was faced.

It was this recognition of their trials and this understanding of the great efforts they were making that caused Hindenburg more and more to earn the gratitude and affection of the whole population of Germany. They did not feel that he was a kind of god, sitting aloof and cold in his high position, for they were made to realize that he really felt with them in their troubles, and that he, like themselves, was working with the utmost of his powers to retrieve the lost fortunes and rebuild a Germany which should be distinguished by a saner, cleaner glory than that of the *Militarismus* period. It counted greatly in his favor, moreover, that he had not accepted the office of President with the idea of satisfying personal ambitions or with the hope of personal gain. He was too old and already too rich in honor and fame to care for these things, and he came to the palace in the Wilhelmstrasse solely with the intention of serving his

PRESIDENT VON HINDENBURG INSPECTING THE GUARD OF HONOUR ON HIS ARRIVAL AT LEIPZIG FAIR

country and his countrymen. And he who had sacrificed his few remaining years of leisure to the public good had the highest right to ask other people to follow his example, and no one could be found in Germany, whether for or against him, who would be inclined to deny him this right.

CHAPTER XXIII

WHEN Germany lost the war, and saw her trade in ruins and her finance in chaos, and when so many material advantages had disappeared, it was scarcely surprising that the professors of the German universities and the learned men throughout the country appealed for help in order that the great traditions of German culture might not also be broken. Fresh blood was needed in the universities, and the sources whence this might have been drawn were sorely depleted. Thousands of young men who had possessed the intellect and the power to perpetuate German learning lay dead in France and in other countries. Thousands more were forced by hard circumstances to make money to support themselves and their families and were therefore unable to spare the time necessary for study. The violent upheavals caused by the war and by the Revolution produced a certain repercussion in the schools and universities, and it seemed likely that their finances would suffer badly and thus still further deplete the slender store of power and energy which remained to them. The new government, however, recognized the need of supporting the seats of learning throughout the country; realizing perhaps, that learning is the one thing of which a man can never be robbed. Money can be taken from him, his credit can be taken from him, and even his fair name and his position may be assailed; but learning once acquired remains the indefeasible possession of its owner, and no violent hands can be laid upon it. The new rulers of the country, therefore, voted what means they could afford to keep life in the schools and universities and to encourage research work in science and art. Local authorities combined with the government in doing what they could to preserve the educational centres and so a good measure of encouragement and security was restored to them. It is safe to say that, had the government neglected this matter, Germany today would not be in the position in which she now stands.

In 1920 all the universities and colleges—all German schools for higher education—bound themselves into an independent, self-administrative corporation, in the hope of preventing the threatened disintegration of German learning and culture. This society,[1] which received the aid of the Kaiser Wilhelm Gesellschaft[2] (in which Hindenburg had taken a great interest since 1900), was very dependent upon the support, both financial and moral, that it would receive from Berlin. The government showed from the very first the keenest desire to do all it could to further the vital work which the *Notgemeinschaft* had undertaken. Among many important matters dealt with by the authorities of the society was the situation of the libraries, which, owing to the years of war, lacked many foreign books. These were promised grants to enable them to complete their collections as early as possible. Many periodicals, also, which were threatened by extinction were preserved by the society, which made it possible for them to continue to be printed. Medical science was helped by grants to obtain the necessary instruments and

[1] *Notgemeinschaft der Deutschen Wissenschaft.*
[2] The Society of Doctors and Natural Science Research Workers.

animals for experimental purposes so that research workers might keep pace with other countries, and even, as the course of medical history has shown, outstrip them. The society went further than this, for it even made possible traveling fellowships and, when it was deemed advisable, assisted explorers and excavators. One of the expeditions which the *Notgemeinschaft* materially helped was the South Atlantic Expedition of 1925, which undertook important deep-sea and air researches for a period of two years.

Ebert, the first German President, did much to further the work of the *Notgemeinschaft,* and Hindenburg, whose association with young people and students had always been so happy, gladly followed along the paths trodden by Ebert.

On June 25, 1925, he received a deputation of students who came to offer him the best wishes of all German students on his election to the presidency. To these young men he addressed the following words of approbation and encouragement for the future of the country:

The student youth of Germany has always possessed my warmest interest, especially because they have suffered so greatly under the difficulties of the last few years. That the fine spirit of Germany is alive in you has been proved by the way in which German students, to a great extent relying upon their own powers, have emerged from the trying years since the war. I know that the time of trouble does not quite yet lie behind us. But what has already been achieved indicates that we shall be able to triumph absolutely. What I can do to help in this work will always be gladly done.

I wish also to express the pleasure it gives me to know that you have come here today as representatives of all German students, and that you are thereby showing that there exists among you a desire to be united and to work together for the good of the country. Protect and strengthen this unity, which is the one foundation stone upon which the future of our people can rest. Always place your country above considerations of party or of opinion, and then you may rest assured that you, the academic youth, will one day see the better future of our people.

A little less than a year later, Hindenburg spoke to the students of the University of Bonn on the occasion of his visit to the recently evacuated Rhine district.

"My age and my office," he said then, in rather wistful tones, "have called me to live and to work among the old; but with you, German youth, I shall hope and believe that you represent the future and the strength of the German nation."

Hindenburg's passionate belief in and love for the children and the youth of his country secured for him everywhere the most enthusiastic reciprocation of his feelings towards them. Professor Lessing, who had not believed "such a degree of childlikeness to be possible," bears eloquent testimony to the effect produced upon the boys under his charge by the words which Hindenburg spoke to them in Hanover. Lessing states that Hindenburg told the children that he would not live to see the rehabilitation of Germany, but that he would look down from Heaven and approve the future deeds of the boys who stood before him. Professor Lessing's words are worth recording:

He really believes that, in all seriousness; after death he will go to God, he will sit on a cloud; he will look down upon Germany from some privileged place in Heaven and will bless my victorious boys. The cheekiest of these, after this "historic experience," drew a picture: Hindenburg, as an angel, floating on a cloud blessing our upper class. It would have been easy to encourage such a mockery; but (and this is remarkable) there was not one among us who did not disdain it as an offence. We felt, it is not knightly, it is mean to fight with weapons of the intellect there, where no kind of possibility or power existed to return the blows with similar weapⁱ

Lessing, in his essay entitled *Hindenburg,* also pays a great tribute to Hindenburg's honesty. At the time when the field marshal was stationed at Oldenburg, Wilhelm Jordan devoted an evening at the literary society to a recitation of part of the *Nibelungenlied.* Hindenburg, having been asked to attend the evening's performance, replied that he had not had time, as a soldier, to occupy himself with literature and that he feared he would be unable to judge of the value of the evening. As Lessing rather dogmatically observes, "a considerable degree of *Barbarei*" [1] is indicated when a German admits that he does not know the *Nibelungenlied,* though he adds that Hindenburg's admission of his ignorance revealed "unusual candor and honesty." Lessing writes further:

But, if one can readily count the books he has read, he has a relationship with the world of art which is remarkable—he collects Madonna pictures; though it is true that it does not matter who painted them or from whence they come. He collects them as others collect stamps, and not at all out of religious feeling; a room in his villa is especially set apart for the reception of Madonna pictures. This fact gives the humane observer all the pleasure that may be derived from the contemplation of a self-sufficing life, narrowly limited and naïvely accepting its limitations.

If Hindenburg, however, was uncultured, he nevertheless appreciated the importance of culture, for the *Notgemeinschaft der Deutschen Wissenschaft* found in him a champion of its cause and a sympathetic and helpful friend in the time

[1] Lack of education.

of trouble. It could hardly be expected that a soldier, and especially so devoted and single-minded a soldier, should also possess academic distinctions and knowledge. The average German professor is only too ready to bestow the epithet *Barbar* upon the unacademic. Only a short time ago, the narrow view taken by a certain type of professor was most neatly demonstrated in an examination. A student, asked to discuss leading contemporary German writers, mentioned among others the name of an author whose name is justly famous not only in his own country but in most others, and who is as much renowned for his prodigious knowledge as for his writing. The mention of this name acted like a draught of powerful evil magic upon the examining professor. In fierce tones, he addressed the unfortunate candidate with the words: "Herr S——, how can you mention that man? Are you not aware that he was unable to pass his matriculation examination?" It is quite certain that the learning of the writer under discussion far exceeded that of the examining professor, and this story must serve to show how it is that a man whose education has been acquired in places other than in the universities comes to be described so brusquely as a "barbarian."

Hindenburg, however, was not indifferent to the importance of education and of learning in general. He spoke at Weimar of the trust and comfort which so many people had been able to find in the heritage of culture which had come down to them through so many generations and which remained undimmed and undisputed at the present day. Not only did the heritage of the past retain its lustre in the eyes of the world, but German intellectual life had survived the storms of war and the darkness of revolution and it was certain that the present leaders of German learning would be able to yield their hold on the reins to a generation which would be worthy to take them over just as they, in their turn, had been fit to accept them from their fathers. The continuity of the intellectual life of the country was thus secured, for, if neither the War nor the Revolution had been able to break it, it seemed unlikely that it would ever pass into nothingness. It cannot be said that Hindenburg personally contributed very greatly to this state of affairs, but he certainly did succeed in impressing upon the academic world, as he tried to do in every other sphere, the necessity of preserving unity and the need that the academic world should not hold itself too coldly aloof, but should try to make its learning a warm and living benefit to the community outside its gates.

In Germany, perhaps more than anywhere else, the postwar *Akademiker*[1] is inclined to take the attitude that the unlearned are "barbarians" and to look upon them as inferior. This is partly to be accounted for by the fact that professors and members of the learned professions have begun to count for more than in the days when the army was everything and all other people nothing. Then, in the hour when they came into their own, the university men were a little inclined to look down upon the rest of the world, and Hindenburg's appeal, that they should not set themselves apart and should always keep in their minds the maxim that the country was to come first and everything else last, was not entirely inopportune. There was some-

[1] Learned man.

thing very touching in the fact that this man, who had lived all his life by the power of the sword, should turn at last to the seats of learning and ask them to educate their young men to help the country in its efforts to recover from the havoc wrought by the sword. That he, who at one time might even have felt a definite approval of a couplet composed by one of the proud dukes of Somerset,[1] should spend the last years of his life in trying to establish in his country the best possible form of democracy was so strange that, in itself alone, this fact was more than sufficient to give his words weight. In his memoirs the words "my Kaiser" constantly appear, and there can be no doubt that he saw in the person of the Emperor almost a god upon earth. In his speeches, after he became President, two other words have been substituted—"our country."

In the universities, the homes of German learning and art, Hindenburg found tradition which had not become obsolete, an hereditary glory of which the most democratic mind could find nothing bad to say. So he, whose own traditions had been so violently torn away from him, turned at last to the great men whose names were renowned in history and who could still wear their crowns and decorations unashamed in the presence of democracy. Of all institutions, Hindenburg looked chiefly to the universities for help and support in achieving his aim. The great "barbarian," therefore, approached the seats of the learned and made his appeal— and shame it had been indeed had he been cold-shouldered at the gates.

[1] "Let laws and learning, arts and commerce die—
But leave us still our old nobility!"

[235]

In the year 1807, when Berlin was occupied by the French, when Prussia was impoverished and politically disturbed, Fichte made his moving addresses to the people and tried to remove their depression and to awaken them to a sense of nationality.   It is strange to note how similar his appeals are to those which Hindenburg, in nearly the same situation, made so many years later.   Fichte said:

> Do not let us say that we must still rest a little longer, still sleep and dream a little longer, until an improvement will, perhaps, set in of itself. It will never come of itself. He, who has once missed yesterday . . . and who even will not arouse himself today, will still less be able to act tomorrow. Every withdrawal only makes us lazier and rocks us more comfortably into a peaceful state of accommodation to our miserable conditions. . . . What is demanded of you is a decisiveness . . . which, without swaying and without tiring, endures utterly until it has reached its goal.

Hindenburg also appealed to the young men of the country, to those within the universities as well as to those without, to answer to a similar call and to make a similar effort to shake off their shackles.   True, his speeches never held that eloquent fire and passion that characterized those of Fichte, but these two utterly dissimilar men came, through the strangeness of circumstances, to do much the same work. Hindenburg, however, did not have to make his appeal to ears so sluggish as those that listened to Fichte; and of all those who came under the sway of Hindenburg's personality none brought him a more eager loyalty, or gave him more willing support, than the university students.   For these he was not simply an old man, but a monument of all the patriotic virtues and a leader who deserved to be obeyed.

His name, even in his lifetime, acquired that magic sound which is usually associated only with the names of those long dead. Living, Hindenburg had become an historical figure and he moved under the golden halo to which his deeds entitled him.

For his military fame, he was entitled to wear the "Blücher-kreuz," but for the still, quiet work he did as President of the German Republic, he wore no outward symbol, and received no reward. But it is more than likely that history will dwell far more upon his achievements after the year 1925 than upon the victories of Tannenberg and the Masurian Lakes, great though these military masterpieces were.

It is not Hindenburg's smallest claim on the gratitude of his country that he succeeded in raising the flame of patriotism in the hearts of the university men. Students in their work very often forget the need for patriotism, and patriotism in those days, moreover, was an outworn word that had latterly fallen into disrepute. To German youth "patriotism" meant something belligerent, and Hindenburg certainly deserves a large share of the credit for reviving that nobler idea of *"Vaterlandliebe"* which was so necessary to the new life of the country.

CHAPTER XXIV

IT was not only necessary for Hindenburg to try to unite the different states in Germany, but he had also to stimulate feelings of patriotism and nationality among the many Germans who lived and worked in foreign countries. The members of the consular service, the many salesmen, students and others who seldom returned to Germany and who were in danger of forgetting that they were German, were helped and encouraged by Hindenburg. Many of these people resented the Revolution and, from their distant places of residence, looked coldly upon the proceedings of the new government. In their eyes, however, the situation improved when Hindenburg became President because he was a representative of the old, discarded traditions. They argued that if he could see promise in the new state of affairs, and if he was content to devote himself to the service of the country under the new régime, then there must be something at least to be said in its favor. Party quarrels grievously divided the Germans abroad, and Hindenburg constantly besought them to remember that upon them rested the responsibility of representing their country in foreign lands and that it was as necessary for them to live and work in harmony as it was for the home-keeping Germans to do so. In many ways Hindenburg showed the interest he took in the troubles of those whose work caused them to live abroad, but this interest was especially revealed by the facts that he became Honorary

President of the Society of Germans Abroad, and that he always welcomed to his house any man whose business kept him in foreign places. By talking to salesmen, artists and others, he drew in a vast store of information and acquainted himself with the many difficulties with which a man may be faced while living permanently in a country other than his own.

There was one dissension which caused widespread bitter feeling among Germans both at home and abroad, but more especially among the latter. This was the *Flaggenstreit.*[1] Many people could not accustom themselves to the new black, red and gold colors and wished to retain the old black, white and red flag. This was a case where the exercise of the greatest possible tact was necessary; for neither those who wished to adopt the new flag whose colors were prescribed by the Constitution of Weimar, nor those who wished to keep the old one at the masthead could be offended. Hindenburg dealt personally with this question, and, on the 5th of May, 1926, an order of the President was published which decreed that the German consular and ambassadorial houses abroad should fly the black, red and gold colors of the Republic and also the black, white and red flag (with black, yellow and red in one corner) of the merchant service. That everything did not, however, run entirely smoothly at first is shown by the following letter of May 9, 1926, which Hindenburg addressed to the chancellor, Dr. Luther:

The second decree of May 5, 1926, with regard to the German flags has met with considerable misunderstanding since it has been made public. The recent trade developments abroad which have

[1] The flag dispute.

smoothed the way towards giving Germany another and better standing in foreign countries, and which are allowing us once more to take a place in world commerce, demand a strong co-operation and a proud recognition of their nationality on the part of all Germans living abroad; and, while these people are living in foreign countries, and working under especially hard circumstances, the unfortunate flag dispute hinders them. The decree was intended to do away with this disharmony, and I am quite certain that it will achieve its purpose.

As I have repeatedly told you, nothing lies further from my mind than to slight in any way the national colors laid down by the Constitution. But, unfortunately, public and press discussions have recently proved once more how dangerous and fatal is a constant dispute about the flag for our people.

It is my sincerest desire to find, as soon as possible, a practicable way in which to provide a satisfactory compromise, which shall meet the requirements of contemporary Germany and its aims, and which shall also be just towards the development and history of our state. I therefore request you to put yourself in communication not only with those who are responsible for our legislation, but also with all societies who are especially interested in this question, so that our aim may be reached with all possible speed. I trust that the time is not far distant when the German people will again be able to live peacefully under one single outward symbol of its nationality.

Thus Hindenburg did not hesitate to take part in the attempts to settle those difficult and delicate problems with which the new state was confronted. It would have been easy for him to skate over these matters with a few vague words, but, wherever he saw that there was anything to be done, he immediately set about doing it. The flag dispute serves simply as an example to show with what tact he approached the burning questions of the day and with what success his efforts were usually attended.

In writing about the President, foreign papers are apt to

stress his military characteristics too much. He has been compared to all kinds of people and to many inanimate objects, and a common verdict has been reached that, were a granite block to be endowed with life, it would be like Hindenburg. No student of human features could be found to endorse a judgment like this. A stiff, upright carriage, a military step, rugged features and a sharp glance—these are the obvious things one notices; but further, the whole face wears an expression of austere kindness which reassures and pleases. True, Hindenburg's typically Prussian personality could never have gained the unreserved love and admiration of an entire people, had it not been for the deeds which had made him famous. It is certain that the Germans as a whole can scarcely see the man for the glamour of his achievements, just as the wooden statue of him that was erected in the Königsplatz in Berlin could in the end scarcely be seen for the nails.[1] It is, however, a most remarkable thing that even those people who have little sympathy with him, personally, find nothing to say against him. *"Ein anständiger Kerl"* [2] is what they are forced to call him, and the tribute of that comment is paid to the President throughout the country.

The Germans who live abroad, however, are most especially grateful to Hindenburg for the personal interest he has taken in them and in their concerns. The flag dispute had touched them more nearly than anything else could have done, and they gladly accepted the solution of the difficulty

---

[1] In order to raise funds for the war, a giant wooden statue of Hindenburg was erected and the public were asked to buy nails which they then hammered into the statue. The monument was called "The Iron Hindenburg."

[2] "A decent fellow."

suggested by Hindenburg, because they looked upon him as a supporter of the good old traditions. To say that he supported the old traditions is perhaps to give a slightly false impression, for it might suggest that he inclined to monarchism and the return of the old army, and this is entirely incorrect. From the day when he stood in the presence of the assembled *Reichstag* and swore the oath of the Weimar Constitution, he never showed the smallest inclination to depart from the precepts of the Republic. He was absolutely loyal to the new Constitution, and did all he could to strengthen and help it. The members of the republican government, too, could never forget how he, the Prussian officer, had thrown the whole weight of his influence into the balance when he brought the soldiers home from France. In these days of gloom and trouble, it was Hindenburg who had saved his country from complete chaos and from Communism.

In January, 1927, the Foreign Germans' Institute, at Stuttgart, celebrated the tenth anniversary of its existence. In honor of this occasion they created the *"Deutscher Ring"* [1] which was to be given to men who deserved the special gratitude of all Germans for the work they had done and which was supposed to be a symbol of the fact that a golden ring of faith encircled all the German people. The first "German Ring" was awarded to Hindenburg and was presented to him as a token of the affection and esteem in which he was held by "foreign" Germans.

Hindenburg also took part in the discussions regarding another bitterly contested question of the day—that of the

[1] German Ring.

"Fürstenenteignung";[1] and his view is revealed in the following letter of May 22, 1926, addressed to the *Staatsminister,* Herr von Lobell:

I have read your letter of May 19 with the liveliest interest. But on legal grounds arising from the constitutional position of President of the German *Reich,* I find myself quite unable to take up a position in a public proclamation with regard to the petition to expropriate the property of the princes. I should also not like to make a decree to the government; for the government, in its announcement of the 26th of April of this year, has already declared, clearly and positively, to the German people that the uncompensated expropriation of properties contradicts the principles which form the basis for every act in a legally administered state. From this standpoint, the government has definitely expressed its objection to the petition for the uncompensated expropriation of the princes' properties, not only in its official announcement but also in the speech of the Minister for Home Affairs in the *Reichstag,* on April 28. The new government formed by the Chancellor, Dr. Marx, on May 17, 1926, has expressly accepted this point of view as its own, in its declaration of May 19. I can therefore assume that the government shares your opinion with regard to the legal consequences and danger of this petition without any special step upon my part being necessary. With regard to the decisions which I myself shall have to make when the matter has advanced further, I must again—as laid down in the Constitution—reserve my decision until after the vote,[2] and until the law based upon that vote is brought to me to be executed.

However, I will not omit to inform you of my personal opinion, and I will state that I fully share the fears which you have expressed; and I have also, from the beginning of the development of this state of affairs, stated to the government the very same considerations as those you adduce. That I, who have passed my life in the service of the Kings of Prussia and the German Kaisers, feel this petition first to be a great wrong and then as revealing a regrettable lack of feeling for tradition and a base ingratitude, I

[1] Confiscation of the property of princes.
[2] *Volksentscheid.*

need hardly tell you. However, I will endeavor to treat the expropriation movement not as a purely political, but as a moral and lawful affair. From this viewpoint, I see in it a considered blow at the vitals of the lawfully administered state, whose deepest foundation is respect for the law and for property which is acknowledged by the law. It strikes a blow against morality and justice. Should this petition find acceptance, one of the pillars upon which the lawfully administered state rests would be cut down and a way cleared which would lead to the expropriation or denial of private property; and which would also lead irresistibly downhill, if a random plebiscite, conducted possibly under stress of strong feeling, were permitted.

Through the precedent of the present case, methods might be adopted to lead the people, by means of irritating popular instincts and exploiting popular needs, still further along the way to the expropriation of private properties, through such plebiscites, and thus to withdraw the basis of Germany's cultural, commercial and social life. I see a great danger in this, especially in our position, which the collective social and moral powers of the nation are absolutely needed to preserve, and I think that our constitutional principles are threatened at a time when we are making our first steps along the road to new commercial importance, and that our position in the world will consequently suffer damage.

I am convinced, in spite of the strong (and in many respects unlovely) agitation for this petition, that the quiet judgment and sound sense of our people will not ignore this moral and legal side of the question, nor fail to recognize the infinite danger that here threatens all classes of people. I therefore confidently hope that our fellow-citizens will bear this in mind in making their decision on June 20, and will avoid the injury that would otherwise be done to the basic principles of every state and the departure from proper administration of the law and of justice.

From this letter it will be seen that the man who had "passed his life in the service of the Kings of Prussia" found it impossible to regard with equanimity the expropriation of the princes' property. As is well known, the princes were finally compensated in money for the expropriation of their possessions, but, of necessity, this compensation fell far short of the value of the lands. Thus, under the shadow of the republican flag, the proud princes of Germany had to suffer the loss of estates which had been in the possession of their families for many generations. The old order had changed, and changed irrevocably. The broad acres passed finally into the hands of the state, to be administered by the people. And the irony of fate had decreed that the man whose signature completed this act of expropriation should be a member of the old order. There must have been bitter feelings in his heart when he was faced with this duty, but there was nothing else for him to do, since he had abandoned all the monarchical principles and accepted the new order, in the hope that this would tend to the final good of the country.

In spite of all that is written about the patriotism that is supposed to flourish in the hearts of all eminent statesmen and soldiers, it is very seldom that this feeling is put to so severe a test as that which Hindenburg's was forced to undergo. And he proved in his whole conduct that for him the country came essentially first, and that beside its claims, those of monarchists or republicans were only minor matters. For this reason, therefore, he was, as President of the Republic, to set aside all personal prejudices, and in fact all other considerations, and to concentrate solely on the rebuilding of the broken house. Politics! The word still sounded unpleasant in his ears; but, in order to achieve his aim, he was obliged to take part in the very affairs which were most distasteful to him.

A much criticised essay,[1] which almost ruined its author's career, and which appeared shortly before the presidential elections, reads as follows:

Here is a perfectly consistent man. I will not speak of the inhumanity and the passionate egoism of his naïve self-righteousness. From the very moment when this least political of men shall be mis-cast in a political rôle, some other man will really do the acting; for this one, through and through, is subservient. In him are not even the beginnings of a personality capable of deciding, measuring and considering. With him the sole criterion will always be tradition, the feeling that "one certainly must," or "one certainly must not." . . . He will remain the "good shepherd and protector" only as long as some clever man is there to interest him in his duties and arrange them for him; given freedom, he would become simply an untamed wolf. A nature like Hindenburg's will ask to the death: "How can I serve?"

It is certainly sad and touching that, during the World War, one of the most evil natures in the history of the world made this simple, trusting man the tool of his ambitions and his desires, and covered his real aims with the flag of national ideals. But just there the danger is revealed! According to Plato, philosophers should rule the people. But a philosopher would hardly mount the throne with Hindenburg. Only a representative symbol, a question mark, a zero, would do that. It may be said "Better a zero than a Nero." Unfortunately, the course of history has shown that behind a zero lurks always a future Nero.

It is not to be denied that there is a certain amount of truth contained in the above sentences. Even if one hesitates to acquiesce in the description of the misguided ex-Kaiser as "one of the most evil men in the history of the world," one cannot dispute that Hindenburg is emphatically a man who has devoted his whole life to "service"; and that a servant is generally guided by a master is also a matter

[1] Professor Theodor Lessing's *Hindenburg*.

about which there is small doubt. Just as Hindenburg was proud to be in the service of the German Kaisers, so, when he became President, he was proud to serve the country. And Professor Lessing goes too far, and shoots very wide of his mark when he states that a Hindenburg, if left to himself, would turn into "an untamed wolf." Possibly Professor Lessing considered that a Prussian soldier, educated and brought up solely with military ideas, could not possibly find either interest or hope in the pursuit of any other business than that of war. This, however, was an erroneous conclusion, as the whole subsequent life of the President has demonstrated. He has not been a party tool. He has kept himself entirely outside party disputes, and he has also, as in the case of the expropriation of the princes' property, not hesitated to express his opinions. He has also loyally kept himself true to the tenets of the republican Constitution, and no criticism could be made of his conduct in the office of President.

Many people will be found to dispute that he is a "strong" man, in the way that Bismarck, for example, was strong. It is certainly true that he does not possess either the force of character or the ruthless will of the Iron Chancellor; in Hindenburg there is more devotion and less ambition. Bismarck had the commanding, trumpet tones of an Isaiah; Hindenburg has the more appealing voice of a John the Baptist, calling for regeneration. Bismarck's achievements were herculean, amazing—but they did not endure. Hindenburg, who expressly writes that a Bismarckian state seems to him to be the ideal one, nevertheless unhesitatingly placed the whole influence of his personality on the side of another type of state altogether. Bismarck worked largely for himself—Hindenburg entirely for the country. Future generations of Germans will certainly remember and honor the name of the less impressive and powerful Hindenburg above the once all-important name of Bismarck. For, in the pages of history Bismarck's work will resemble simply a flash in the pan, the·result of which scarcely outlasted his lifetime. It will be contended, "But he was the first to unite the German states and form them into an Empire." The reply is that he united the German states by wielding his powers unscrupulously, and he united them not upon a basis of mutual understanding, but by means of subordinating them to Prussia. Had he really succeeded, revolution would have knocked in vain at the gates of the Empire—a united people would have clung to the monarchy it had been trained to honor.

Hindenburg is the right man in the right place. He has to some extent succeeded in uniting the country by implanting his own ideals in the hearts of many of his countrymen. He has the gift of making high and low feel "I too am a German, I will do what I can for Germany." At the death of Ebert, the country needed a popular figurehead, someone at the helm who meant something personally to every man, woman and child in the country. And a curious chance made a soldier the head of a pacifist land, a monarchist the President of a Republic, an old man typify the hopes and ambitions of a very young state. It is also not a little remarkable that not one man in the ranks of the new government could be found who was really fitted to be its head.

CHAPTER XXV

THE 2nd of October, 1927, Hindenburg's eightieth birthday, gave the whole nation an opportunity to show its gratitude to and admiration of its soldier President. The question of how best to express those feelings was discussed at a cabinet meeting, and, as a result, the following announcement was made public on June 21:

At one of its recent meetings, the cabinet considered the question of the best way to celebrate the eightieth birthday of President von Hindenburg on October 2, this year. It is clear that the German people are determined to take the opportunity given to them on this occasion of once more expressing their affection and respect for him. On the other hand, the government is convinced that it is acting according to the wishes of the President if it refrains from organizing expensive, general celebrations on this day, and rather casts the birthday wishes in a form appropriate to present needs and to the distress which still exists among our people. In order to give every German, both at home and abroad, an opportunity to express the grateful honor in which he holds the person of the President, the *Reichs* government and the local governments of the various German states have decided to inaugurate a "Hindenburg Fund," which shall be handed to the President on his eightieth birthday. We are certain that the President's wishes will be met if we suggest to him that the sum collected be applied for the benefit of those who stand particularly high in his affections, namely, the wounded, and the relatives of the fallen. Besides the collection of subscriptions for this purpose, which is to be carried out with the aid of the great business houses, etc., the issue of a Hindenburg postage stamp has been considered. This is to give wider circles of people a chance to take part in giving a birthday present to the President. Its proceeds are preferably to be devoted to the relief of distressed middle-class people, pensioners, etc.

This announcement met with the widest approval, and subscriptions soon began to reach the collecting centres from all parts of Germany and from abroad. It was said that this form of honoring the President did credit equally to him and to the people of Germany. It would have been simple to arrange a general holiday with all the usual fireworks and displays which are so dear to German hearts, but this idea—to refrain from expensive celebrations—was far more appropriate to the occasion and far more pleasing to Hindenburg himself. The sum which could be collected thus was, of course, small if weighed in the balance against the terrible distress still existing in Germany. Indeed, as witnessed by the continually recurring riots of Communists, in whose ranks may be found many unemployed and miserable people, there is still much suffering in Germany. It cannot, however, be expected that the awful effects of a World War could be cleared up in a few years. That Germany is, on the whole, a peacefully administered and properly organized country is very much to the credit of a great people, which has really only just awakened to the fact that it is a people at all. For too many years, there was no national feeling in the country, but only a kind of awed *Begeisterung* [1] for the powers that reigned, coupled with a terrible, patient acquiescence in the organization to which all classes of people were subjected. At the head of the administration of all affairs of state were the militarists, and their powers were very

[1] Enthusiasm.

IN THE GARDEN OF THE PRESIDENT'S PALACE, WILHELMSTRASSE, BERLIN

nearly absolute, subject always, of course, to the will of the Kaiser.

"This Germany," writes Stresemann,[1] "collapsed as a result of the World War. It broke in its constitution, in its social uses and in its commercial shape. Its thoughts and feelings have been re-formed. No one can say that this reformation has yet reached its end. It is a process that will continue through many generations. But haste and unrest are symptoms in our modern life, and development moves at greater speed than it has ever done before. *At the heart of this development is the question: how far it is necessary and possible to be national in this developing process, and how far the process is led, determined and hampered by international facts, powers and ideas.*"

In this last sentence, Stresemann approaches the most burning question which has confronted modern German statesmen. It has been variously answered.

Hindenburg's feelings on this subject have already been clearly defined. "We must stand well with foreign countries, but we must achieve friendly relations with them by showing that we are a great nation, that we are worthy of all honor, and that we are capable of rising from the wreck of the war; and not by a pallid policy of conciliating them at any price." This view, from which he never deviated, was the only one that could properly be taken by a statesman who could really see into the future. No country could hope to climb to eminence in the world by adopting a method of ingratiation. Ingratiation serves, at best, as a poor, temporary makeshift for one who has no courage to take a

[1] *Der Deutsche Weg.*

bolder course, but, as any sort of ground principle it is as futile as it is feeble.

Before the presidential elections, the question was often asked: "What can such an old man expect to achieve?" On the occasion of his eightieth birthday, the triumphant admirers of this "old man" were able to point to the enormous work he had done, both to improve matters at home and to re-establish the credit of Germany in the eyes of the world. The voices of those who had doubted him were silenced, or else were raised to join in the chorus of acclamation which was heard on all sides. Surely it can seldom have occurred in the history of the world that a soldier has stood before a war-weary nation as the symbol of its achievements in the time of peace.

Perhaps the feelings of the whole German nation towards its President are most aptly expressed in the speech made in his honor, on the occasion of his eightieth birthday, by Dr. Guenther-Holstein in the town hall of Greifswald.

Must we not all approach him as pupils? Around him our contemporaries restlessly plan and talk, and alas! never come to deeds—but he acts; and what he does is duty, what he practices is faith, and what he carries is responsibility. What would appear to be the Spirit of the Age plays its superficial games and throws its gleaming crowns into the air, which, if one tries to catch them, break like soap-bubbles in the sun—but he is silent and listens to the deep heartbeat of all things, and sees in everything the sacred, eternal and moral powers with which alone true creative work may be done. Around us, so many unskilled people stare at the Fata Morgana of a future which simply gives back an image of their own dreams—but he knows that everything new, which is to last, can arise only upon the basis of nationality, that nationality which has grown out of history, which comes into existence through history, and which can never be released from history.

. . . When the German people elected Hindenburg to be their leader, they paid their tribute to history. For the history of a people is not something outward that one can put off like a garment, and then regard as past and gone, as one might put into a museum some relics that from then on are simply looked upon like outgrown children's shoes or toys, which are of no use any more. But history is like the strong roots of a tree; the winds of today hasten through its branches and the sap pulses through its leaves and fruit; but this life-giving sap rises from the roots and, through it, the leaves become green and the fruit ripens. One of the greatest German thinkers has well said: "History is always the present." For the present is nothing but a channel through which the stream of history flows to us from the past, in order, through us, to pass farther into the future. For what works in history is nothing else than the great spiritual powers which it carries, and, as they work creatively upon us, so they will work creatively upon the future.

. . . When the German people elected Hindenburg, it admitted the morality of its whole history, admitted in particular the morality of its war, which it had waged with the whole of the heavy, ethical seriousness that is characteristic of the Germans. What did we know of the many confusions, what of the play and interplay of diplomatic skill and unskilfulness, which always veil with thick webs every turning-point of the world's history? We only know, as Fichte knew a hundred years ago, that our struggle was concerned with the preservation of the whole of our physical and spiritual being and was therefore a moral duty and, to us, a holy war. Because the German is so serious a man and so utterly led by his conscience, nothing has so deeply wounded and distressed him as the lying reproach of war-guilt, but, for this reason also, nothing has acted so consolingly and purifyingly upon him as the word spoken by Hindenburg upon the battlefield of Tannenberg. And, therefore, we shall not let the eagle flight of this word be lost among the frightened cries of the many faint-hearted who sit by the wayside. . . .

When Kaiser Wilhelm I celebrated his ninetieth birthday, more than a generation ago, the writer, Ernst von Wilderbruch, in whose veins flowed the blood of the same proud race, sent the exulting sentence, "We have him still!" through the whole of Germany. The same sentence is on our lips today. We still have him, he is still with us, the mighty old man with the iron-grey hair and the large, quiet features, who is now passing into the ninth decade of his life. How many, in these fearful years since the war, have sunk into oblivion, broken in body and soul, even after they had faithfully done their utmost until the end of the war! But he still stands as upright as ever. . . . We still have him—but what will happen when he is no longer here? The problems we have to face are still gigantic. Germany is still split in twain by two classes which represent the strongest social antithesis, the parties still dispute as bitterly and inconsiderately as ever, and, beyond the boundaries, millions of our countrymen are tragically fighting for their nationality. Truly, who is there among us who will not raise his hand and swear that he will not rest until we are once more a socially united people, until that time comes when each man shall see the other only as his brother; a people who are one in a firm national will; a people with one idea—to stand by their brothers on the other side of the frontier, united in deed and sacrifice. Ah! it is easy to swear an oath on some high day or holiday, but the work of ordinary days is so difficult; and before the veil of the future even the bravest man may feel his stout heart trembling.

. . . Thus we come to the man who today is the protector of our state. We do not clap our hands, we cry no hurrahs. What there is in our hearts of gratitude and rejoicing may find its expression only in the sound of music. But we will allow our song of Germany to be heard too, our avowal of Germany, an avowal which is not only upon our lips but in the depth of our hearts. Germany, my sacred country, if I forget thee, then let my own rights be forgotten!

Thus Dr. Guenther-Holstein stresses the urgent need for unity and recognizes as Hindenburg's greatest glory the work he has done in this direction. The speech was delivered more than two years ago, and, fortunately for Germany, he is still alive and still in office.

Hindenburg is characterized by the "heavy German seriousness" to which Dr. Guenther-Holstein refers. He is in fact almost more heavy and more serious than most Germans, and we find in him little of wit or of humor. His speeches and letters are all couched in the same unadorned language that one associates with military men. He is almost uncompromisingly plain in what he says—it would seem as if he despises the words he is obliged to use, and so unskilled is he in the art of speech that he does not fully realize the effect that may be produced by a word in season. From a very early age, he has preferred deeds, and has found more satisfaction in fulfilling a job than in discussing what might best be done. His motto "Ora et labora" left him little time to acquire eloquence.

The gift presented to him by the nation on his eightieth birthday met absolutely with his approval. No present could have given him greater pleasure. The wounded soldiers and the distressed relatives of the fallen had occasion to be thankful that he was of such a character as to find this the most acceptable gift.

The whole of Germany made haste to do Hindenburg honor on this birthday; each different state did what it could to contribute to the fund, for they all felt that Hindenburg, for all his constant labor in the cause of unity, nevertheless did not wish to rob them of their own peculiar characteristics and habits.

So it was that on October 2, 1927, the old President received a gift which represented the united affections of the whole of Germany and which was a tribute paid to him by those Germans who lived in foreign places as well as those who lived at home.

CHAPTER XXVI

WE have come at last to the end. In the foregoing chapters the course of Hindenburg's life has been traced from his infancy to his ripe old age; from an undistinguished boyhood to the highest military glory, and from thence to the presidency.

There will be found many to question whether he is a genuinely great man; who will point, in support of their arguments, to his Prussian narrowness of vision and to what Lessing has called his "naïve egoism." It will be said that a man so hedged in by the boundaries of his traditions and education, and so apparently unconscious of his limitations, really deserves (whatever he may have achieved) to be called a figurehead. It will be stated that Hindenburg is not a man of ideas, and that he can walk only in appointed paths.

And all this, to a large extent, is true. Hindenburg is not, like Bismarck, a man of ideas. Bismarck had the power not only to evolve ideas, but to put them into execution. He was the first to make a united Germany possible; he alone created the Empire. Fate then overthrew his work and plunged it into hopeless ruin—and there was no new Bismarck found in Germany to restore it. It must never be forgotten that Bismarck was the first to unite these states, or what a herculean task the forming of that union was. But the work that he did was nevertheless not stable, and we venture to think that the work of Hindenburg will have more lasting results. The idea upon which he is working is still, broadly speaking, the idea of Bismarck; but the method is far different. Hindenburg tries everywhere to conciliate and to improve the conditions of all classes of society. He has sacrificed his own soul for the sake of the country; in his old age he has come forward and, by the light of a personal example, he has led his people through some of the darkest and most difficult years that any country has ever been called upon to endure.

What is needed by a people in a transition stage is a moral support, and such support is perfectly supplied by natures such as Hindenburg's. From the day when he shamefacedly brushed the tears away from his eyes so that the new cadet's jacket might not be disgraced, he had schooled himself never to give way under whatever blows fortune might deal him. Now, in his eighty-third year, he carries himself as upright as an oak-tree and fulfils unswervingly all the manifold duties of his high office. There are many people in Germany today who might be disposed to give way under the strain of living, who might be glad to quit the scene of action and retire with what they can get to some quiet·corner, but who are restrained from taking such a course by the memory of a tired old man who still carries on, who does his job quietly, and who has appealed to every soul in the country to help him in the great task of rebuilding the national house.

"The German people," he once said, "have lost faith in themselves. We cannot allow ourselves to give way to these moods of renunciation. No nation can desert its place in the great world-competition to advance and ennoble humanity." At the time of Hindenburg's eightieth birthday, conditions in Germany were far from good. There were still strained relations between the Left and the Right parties; attempts were still being made to force insufficient means to do the work of a proper fiscal balance. There was still no clarity in regard to aims, nor did any clear policy exist. All that could be done was to try to carry on, to make half a loaf do in place of a whole one, to make five small fishes feed a multitude. And, unfortunately, the men in power were no miracle-workers, and were not even able to concentrate freely on home and foreign policy, because for the most part they were torn, by party strife and internal disharmony among themselves, from the quiet consideration and solution of the difficulties of the day.

Hindenburg, in the meantime, sat in his high place and simply did with his might what lay nearest to him, what demanded to be done. His keen eye missed nothing; not the smallest cross-current of the day escaped his attention, and he gave due weight to all that he saw and heard. And he went on working, quietly and silently; and he has finally succeeded in building up that policy which is known as the *"Hindenburg Linie,"* that policy which said "everything for the country and nothing for the party," and which demanded action and remedy for bad conditions, rather than discussions and meetings. Today it seems possible that, through the great personal efforts made by Hindenburg, Germany may be able to escape from the unenviable political situation in which she is placed. Hindenburg was able to combine a strong home policy of reconciliation w.... sane handling of foreign affairs. Previously, there had seemed to be no middle course; everyone was either a "conciliate-the-foreigner" or a violently "national" partisan. Different tendencies and political opinions were sending the country deeper and deeper into chaos and ruin. It was Hindenburg's essential sanity that so greatly helped to restore to the country something at least of her lost balance. As has already been seen, too, Hindenburg's influence was not confined to one class of people: he stood equally high in the regard of everyone; and to him personally may be traced the greater assurance that may now be found in the conduct of affairs both at home and abroad. Through him personally, many people who had been bitterly hostile to the new government were won over to do what they could to heal the existing internal differences rather than to increase them. He has been a kind of symbol of hope for the future, and through his speeches and writings he has managed to restore some feeling of nationality, some new vigor, into the general social life throughout the country.

Germany today has to deal also with constantly recurring Communist riots. These riots do not consist simply of meetings and red-flag songs, nor do they end with a few broken windows; instead, they always assume a most alarming form. A few shots at least are always fired, and usually a pitched battle takes place between the police and the rioters. Harmless pedestrians are frequently wounded and killed, and the police handle the situation with such rigor that, in the affected districts, more bitterness is felt towards them than towards the Communists.

The reason why Communism has assumed such grave proportions in Germany is cumulative. Long before the War, Bismarck had had high words with the young Kaiser Wilhelm II because the latter had heard of the distressing conditions under which some striking miners were living, and wished to investigate the matter. Bismarck was in favor of shooting the strikers, as an example to other workers not to abandon their *"Pflichtgefühl"* [1] in this manner. To this word, which was constantly forced upon the notice of the people, may be traced the beginning of the trouble. The workers were not supposed to want anything, were not expected to have desires or feelings. They were to work simply out of a sense of duty, and to hope for no reward. Holidays were few and far between, and, in pre-war days, the shops were open even on Sundays. The workers were expected to do their job and to ask for nothing else than to work for the sake of the work. In return, on an average, the people were certainly better housed, better clothed and better fed than the workers of any other country. The general standard of education was also higher in Germany than elsewhere. But the iron shadow of this *"Pflichtgefühl"* lay over everything and everybody, and, it was small wonder that the workers began, little by little, to ask for their share of the good things of life and for a chance to be happy. It is also not surprising that Communism began to be a serious danger, after the Revolution. War always leaves behind it a trail of abnormal conditions, and a beaten country feels these more heavily than a victorious one. Had Germany won, victory could have served only to fix the Kaiser more firmly on his throne and to give the army a more shining name

[1] Feeling of duty.

among the civilian population. But, when the country was starved and defeated, there was nothing and nobody that the population could trust. Small wonder, when they looked back upon the years of disciplined repression to which they had been subjected, and remembered the four ghastly years of war from which they had emerged, that they rose and threw off the repression of the old government. It was also not unnatural that extremes of feeling should exist—Communism and monarchism; and it must at once be admitted that of these two extremes Communism is the stronger. There are very few people in Germany today who would welcome the return of the Kaiser and a militarist régime. Many of those who would have done so have been won over from their uncompromising attitude towards the new government by the fact that Hindenburg has become President. If he, whose name was so closely bound up with the monarchy and with the old army, could see the advantages in this new form of government, could see in it a hope for the future of the nation, then they too must be prepared to give it a trial. The Communists consist chiefly of the unemployed and the unskilled laborers, whose pay is poor, and it must be admitted that these people have a genuine grievance. There is much suffering among them, and it is no difficult matter to inflame them against the state and against the police, who do not hesitate to fire upon them. In the excitement of the moment the police are very undiscriminating, and a story has been told of how a Berlin Chief of Police, in plain clothes, became involved in a Communist riot, and was severely knocked on the head by a constable. Needless to relate, the constable responsible for this deed of desecration was never found, but there was considerable dismay in the police force over the affair.

Hindenburg himself does all he can to conciliate the extremist factions in Germany. He does not speak of "*Pflicht-gefühl*" to men who are starving. He says, "I know the difficulties under which you are struggling. We are doing what we can to remedy them, and we ask you to help us as far as you can for the sake of the country. It is our desire to leave Germany in a better condition for our heirs, and we can do this only if we all work together, and try to see the whole picture and not just the little corner of it that affects ourselves."

Thus it comes about that Hindenburg is not unsympathetically regarded even by the Communist extremists, because he has sufficient breadth of vision to recognize that they are making heavy weather and are suffering almost more than anyone else from the unfavorable economic conditions.

Matters are now slowly, slowly improving. True, there is still a deceptive appearance of prosperity in such places as Berlin. Thousands of prosperous-looking shops and cafés daily open their doors to streams of customers. Many of the former are living on credit, while the latter change hands perhaps three times a year, as owner succeeds owner along the path to the bankruptcy courts. Businesses cut their expenses down to the narrowest possible margin and offer their goods at the cheapest rates in order to make sales. Credit is long and money is tight, and everyone knows that it will probably be years before there is any real improvement. The enormous burden of war debts rests crushingly upon the shoulders of the country and everyone has to carry his share. No one can withhold admiration from a country which has so gallantly tackled the problems of its own rehabilitation while bearing so heavy a weight of debt at the same time. What Germany has done in these years since the war, including the restoration of the financial situation after the inflation period, has been the result of the most herculean labor on the part of the government and the people. This enormous struggle has left the country tired and dried up, and has disheartened everyone. Nerves are stretched to the utmost, and political tension still runs high throughout Germany.

But above the tumult and fret of everyday life, above the actions and counter-actions of the parties, stands the President. He alone sounds the note of hope and encouragement, he alone keeps the whole country, in a certain measure, united. His has, indeed, been "a strange and wonderful fate," for it has fallen to his lot to see the founding of the German Empire, to stand among the distinguished officers at Versailles for the *Kaiserproklamation*, and to pass from the highest military honors to the highest civil position in his country.

"War is the normal condition for a soldier," he had, as a young lieutenant, written to his parents. Perhaps this idea has never wholly left him, but he has come to realize that wars may be waged without guns and bloodshed. "Peace hath her victories no less renowned than war," and it has been the task of the soldier to wrest for his country some victories of peace from the battles of time. "Courage!" is his cry to the youth of Germany, that youth which has grown up under such different conditions from those which he knew

as a young man. But it is German youth—it represents the
new truth which opposes "ancient error." Hindenburg, perhaps, cannot quite bring himself to admit that the old order
was really in error because he was too closely identified with
it. In 1920, he was still able to write that a state run according to Bismarckian principles seemed to him to be the best,
and he, who had seen Bismarck at the height of his triumph,
at the moment when his dream of empire became fact, could
never forget the great man, and had always in his mind the
knowledge that Bismarck had achieved the union of the German states at a time when the existence of the princes had
made such union a most difficult and delicate task. Yet he
had succeeded; and years afterwards, Hindenburg followed
in his footsteps so far as this basic idea was concerned, and
tried to reunite all the states, from which, however, the
princes had been driven. Hindenburg, like Bismarck, has
his dream, which is to bring not only all the states, but all
classes of people, into the closest union and co-operation.
He places the same value upon the clerk as upon the owner
of the business, if only each does his job with all the strength
of which he is capable. To him, there is nothing higher
than the performance of duty, and, today he holds the same
view which he expressed in his *Aus meinem Leben,* in 1920:
"No citizen possesses any right which does not carry with it
a duty of equal weight." Of him it must be admitted by
everyone that he has never refused any duty, however, trifling
it might be, nor withheld his attention from the dull details
of routine which so many people simply allow to slide.

From one point of view, the Germans are a strangely
tragic people. The many difficult periods of unrest and

distress through which they have had to go have scattered them throughout the world. There are, in all countries, people of German extraction who have taken themselves and their labor to other lands than their own, and who, because they are so adaptable, have simply settled in the places of their adoption and have lost their German nationality. The Germans were always welcome colonists owing to their untiring industry and their powers of building up something from nothing. There is hardly another nation in the world that has so many countrymen scattered in other countries. It has always been a great concern to Hindenburg that those Germans who are forced today by their business to live in foreign countries shall not forget their own, and shall continue to carry in their hearts an intimate consciousness that they are Germans. It is for this reason that he is always so glad to welcome to his house any man who lives and works abroad and to hear something about the conditions under which these distant countrymen of his are existing. His message to "foreign" Germans is always the same. "The other countries in which you work may be great, powerful and beautiful, but they are not Germany."

Like Fichte, Hindenburg tells the people not to grow careless and simply become accustomed to bad conditions of living, but to work that these may be improved; and the people answer his call as best they may. But the work required is not only "long, quiet and peaceful"—it is uphill and laborious, and the results are very slow in appearing.

It is hard for us today to reach a just estimate of what Hindenburg, the stiff old soldier, has done for Germany, and it will be for future generations to determine correctly just how far his work has gone along the paths he wished it to go. Today, his countrymen affectionately call him *"der Vater des Volkes"* [1] and the name is not inappropriate. His age and fame entitle him to the veneration of the young, which is whole-heartedly given him through the length and breadth of the land: the savior of Prussia; the man whose influence alone preserved the army from revolting at the end of the War; the man who, finally, in the face of adverse criticism at home and open hostility abroad, accepted the seat of President, silenced all the enmity expressed towards him, and has done more than any other living man to give Germany back her place in the world. For this reason alone it should be acknowledged that this "least political of men" is the first man of his country living today. There are certainly men more skilled than he in the conduct of affairs, men with a wider horizon and a greater eloquence; but there is about Hindenburg something rock-like, steady and still, which has acted reassuringly and healingly on the distracted people. That Hindenburg should now possess the trust and respect of the whole country is scarcely surprising, but that he should have possessed it in sufficient measure to give him the office of President at the elections is a matter which needs some probing to make it clear. The country had reacted violently against the old form of government, against *Militarismus* and against all its supporters. In this reaction, one name alone retained its lustre—the name of Hindenburg. Everyone knew that had the old field marshal left his post in the hour when the monarchy fell, there would have been none to restrain the returning armies, none to organize the

[1] The people's father.

demobilization. "I remained at my post," writes Hindenburg, and he superintended the whole gigantic work of disbanding the troops· and seeing that the proud warriors of the old army went quietly to their homes. He stayed at his post and saw them go, and he must have felt as if the whole world lay in ruins about him, for they were disappearing for ever and were taking their honors into the quiet of their homes. He who had been so proud of his soldiers was obliged to bid them go, and, soon after, he followed them into retirement. Few will be found to dispute that this was one of the greatest armies the world has ever seen, and yet, at the time when the war finished, it had small honor in its own country. The war-distracted people had ceased to look upon soldiers as heroes, and the "romance" of fighting was no longer romance. We wish to repeat here that, in so far as Hindenburg was a supporter of militarist ideas, he had some justification for giving his support to the army. He knew what the soldiers had endured in the trenches, and how hard it had been for them to fight on while they realized that only a spirit of sullen discontent existed in their homes. And the great hearts of the soldiers were something that their leader could never forget, and though he is the President of a pacifist country, he never has forgotten it. This man, who was a soldier, still loves the men of the old army, still does all he can to help them in their civil life. These were they who kept the foot of the enemy out of Germany—how should he forget them? And he trusts to the spirit of the old army to restore the prestige of the country. His most eloquent words plead with the people to do as much for Germany as those did who fell on the battle-fronts, and his constant exhortations to the youth of the country always contain the words: "Be worthy of your fathers." It is the highest he can ask of them.

Hindenburg as field marshal was a martinet, a man of iron with regard to matters of duty, a man whom his juniors respected and liked, but whose displeasure they certainly feared. As President, he has revealed himself as a deeply human man, to whom the distress of his country is as a personal grief to himself. He has devoted his whole life to its service, and it almost seems as if the honors that have fallen to his share mean nothing to him. He is that most rare type of man who works simply from a sense of duty and who has no thought of reward. His highest satisfaction is the realization of work well done. He can almost be compared to Longfellow's village blacksmith, that man who worked for the joy of working, who owed no man anything, and who went to bed at night knowing that he had earned his night's repose.

It is a dull type of man; sober, religious and unpassionate. In the life story of a great man, we like to read of spectacular deeds, of how he has trodden a shining pathway to eminence. All the better if he starts in an obscure place—for the contrast between his beginning and his end is the more dramatic. But of Hindenburg we cannot say that his life or his character is spectacular. He has followed the plain path of his duty, and has wielded an immense influence over his countrymen at a time when such an influence as his was sorely wanted. He has given moral support when there was no one else to supply it. He is fortunate in that he is the right man in the right place at the right moment. Too often, we hear that this or that genius was born out of his time and his work has never come to fruition. Hindenburg was born at the right moment—it is improbable that, had the course of events run more peacefully, his name would ever have been known. In the year of the outbreak of war he was simply a retired general, and now he is the first man in his country. And all this fame and the greatest part of his life's work came to him after retirement. He certainly little thought, when he went to his house at Hanover in 1911, that the best of his life lay before him or that in a few years' time he himself would be the popular idol of the people. Yet, so it has turned out.

People have compared Hindenburg to all the great German military men—and these have been many—and have found points of resemblance between him and each of these historic characters; and, indeed, he does seem to have combined in himself the highest military qualifications of many of them, and he certainly possesses the "simplicity" of character which appears to have been part of the nature of every great soldier. Hindenburg has been compared even to Napoleon, though here, we must confess, we can see little similarity. Napoleon was everything that Hindenburg is not. Napoleon was a man whose greatness was not of his time; he would have risen to eminence at any period of the world's history. Napoleon, too, was the pure egoist, who sought everything for himself and whose own desires counted for more than anything else. And Napoleon was as spectacular as a shooting star, while Hindenburg is a very "plain, blunt man," with none of the Corsican's brilliance.

Hindenburg is one of those "famous men of little showing," whose work continues long after they have ceased to exist, whose harvest is great beyond their knowing. As Hindenburg stands at the head of the government and the people, there is little doubt that he sees more clearly all that remains to be done in the time to come than the measure of what has already been achieved. He sees the riots and the miserable conditions that cause them, he sees party pit itself against party in a strife which is not unmixed with self-seeking. He sees the tumult, the insecurity, the fierce partisanship which is to be found among all classes of the people. It must look to him as if his appeals for unity and singleness of purpose have fallen on deaf ears—but, for all that, his work lives vitally, and he has gone farther than he probably realizes along the road towards his goal. And all that he has done has been achieved simply by his personal example, for he is not a man of great intellectual powers nor is he distinguished by any outward brilliance. He has, however, a fixed aim, and he has worked quietly and tirelessly to reach it and has not deviated by a hair's breadth from his chosen path. In all his life, nothing has tempted him to forsake his duty, and this is the reason why there is only respect for his name even among those classes of the people who were against his election. Professor Lessing's fear that a great soldier would be "mis-cast for a political rôle" has not been justified; for proof is everywhere visible that there could have been no better President than Hindenburg.

In 1929, Hindenburg wrote a short introduction to a book (*Deutsche Einheit Deutsche Freiheit*) which was published in honor of the tenth anniversary of the establishment of the

Weimar Constitution. This preface shows once more, as all his writings and all his speeches show, that he still works to achieve the union of the country and that his hopes for the future are in the youth of Germany. The preface reads as follows:

No other people has had to wrestle so fiercely for outward freedom and inward unity as the German. The country, situated in the heart of Europe, with unprotected boundaries on all sides, has always been too easily attacked by foreign powers. Only by means of bitter fighting have we been able to preserve our independence, and only in the last century, after a long period of disunion, was it possible to lay the foundations for German nationality. The strong determination of the German people to be united and free has held the state together, even through the storm of the World War and the misery of the post-war time. The German people, in sacrificial devotion, has worked its way back to the light, through the internal troubles and outward oppression that a hard peace has brought upon us.

The conditions which our country needs to preserve its unity and freedom are self-confidence towards the other countries and unity at home. May the present generation, and above all the growing youth, learn from the past and from the trials of the time in which they live! Then they will know how to cherish and to inspire with new life the unity and freedom which their fathers earned in such severe struggles.

VON HINDENBURG

These words bear the conviction of complete sincerity; they are simple sentences, indeed, but they go home to the hearts of the people to whom they are addressed. No one who has not been in Germany for a considerable period can have the least idea of how disruptive an effect the Revolution has had upon the country and just how much the "troubles of the present day" have affected all the people from the lowest to the highest. In Germany, only a few years ago, the old saying "Every man for himself and the devil take the hindermost" was peculiarly appropriate. It certainly applied to all political parties, and the insidious gospel spread from them to the people. Finally, the voice of Hindenburg was raised, and he said "For the country, I would allow both my hands to be cut off; but for the party—nothing!" Here was a strong word in season, coming from the mouth of a man whose patriotism had been proved before all the world, against whose good faith no word could be said. The people listened when he spoke, at first because they venerated this almost legendary old man, and then because they realized that his words contained a vital truth. Poor Germany, torn into pieces by almost every kind of political, economic and moral dissension, listened to the voice which commanded her to cease strife and to try instead to regain her old place in the world.

It is often said that the child is father to the man, but Hindenburg seems to be an illustration, in this case, of the exception that proves the rule. He left his school, for instance, with a report which, though in the main good, accused him of a tendency to "chatter"! This was actually written of a man who in later life never spoke an unnecessary word, and in association with whose name the word "chatter" has a ridiculous sound. He was fairly industrious on the whole, but he was not uniformly hard-working, for, in the same report from school, we find that "his industry has recently decreased." There are plenty of lazy boys in Germany, but there are also many whose one aim seems to be to pass through their schools with the utmost credit to themselves. Somehow one would expect, from the military and the later record of Hindenburg, that he would have been found among these. It is refreshing, therefore, to find that he chattered and was not constantly bending over his books, for, much as is to be read about his geniality, we are unable to find many traces of it in the story of his life. This is due, to some extent, to the facts that he seldom unbends in public and that his whole nature is so typically Prussian— that is to say, he is sober, without passion, and tremendously self-disciplined. We have elsewhere repeated a story which has a great claim to fame—for it tells us of the only occasion when Hindenburg was known to laugh on duty. It is a relief to us to know that he did laugh on that one occasion —for we feel that his life's history is an unnaturally solemn one. In the story of almost every other great man, we can hear of little, silly anecdotes to relate, so that the picture presented is not one of unrelieved greatness—but in Hindenburg's we cannot find many such. He is a serious man, who has carried, in his time, a greater weight of responsibility than almost any living human being. It is his glory that he was great enough to accept this responsibility and that he has not failed anywhere. It is not fair to regard him simply as an animate rock, for he is a man who has deeply felt the hard fate of his country, and who has revealed a sensitive understanding of the needs of the present day.

It is very easy to be witty at the expense of such a type of man as Hindenburg. He is quite unable to defend himself against such attacks as that made upon him by the cheeky boy in Professor Lessing's class in the Hanover school. It is easy to sneer at Hindenburg's so-called naïveté and child-likeness, at his intellectual *"Barbarei"* and his heavy serious-

PRESIDENT VON HINDENBURG ABOUT TO CELEBRATE HIS SIXTIETH
MILITARY JUBILEE

ness. But we should feel it an ignoble form of amusement,
and we should not feel that we had come off victorious even
though he remained inarticulate and helpless under our
humorous sallies. Hindenburg's sure defence against this
type of "baiting" is his simplicity and sincerity. We think
we are justified in calling Hindenburg a great man despite
his obvious limitations. We are not speaking now of what
he has accomplished, for, as previously indicated, we are not
yet in a position to judge exactly how long his work will
last. We refer now to the man himself, and we find an
intrinsic greatness in his character. He is a strong man,
in that he has entirely cast off his original prejudices, at an
age when most men are too rigidly set in their mental habits
to be able even to consider a change. He is a great man
because he subordinated himself to a new régime for the
sake of the country, and certainly by so doing he saved
immeasurable distress.

And now, since 1925, he has held the post of President,
and has fulfilled the manifold duties of his office with great
honor to himself. He is the idol of the people, *"Vater Hindenburg,"* and he stands for all that was best in the old
order. The young republic, having finally thrown off the
former government, has yet heeded Hindenburg's appeals to
it not to forget what it owes to the past. Tradition
is a great, fine-sounding word, and it must not be lightly
regarded as old-fashioned and musty. A people cannot
escape from its traditions simply by driving away its kings
and princes. Hindenburg, an old man, "too old to believe
in sudden changes," with all the weight of his tradition
behind him, has nevertheless been the man who has shown

new Germany her appointed path. He, with his old, experienced eyes, saw the way through the tangle of present-day affairs, and he was the first to show how the way might be cleared. "Germany has lost her belief in herself—but I have never lost my faith in the German people. I know that they will once more occupy their old, honorable place in the world."

Hindenburg! The name is solid and heavy, like the character of its owner; but we think that when the history of the present has become old this is the name that will be most honored. Alfred Niemann, in his *Hindenburg,* tells a story of how a French princess passed through the German capital on a journey. She left the train and took her children to look at the "Iron Hindenburg" in the Königsplatz.

"Regardez," she said to them, *"c'est un homme! Souvenez vous en toujours."*

The French lady was right in her estimate, and we think her words make a very just ending to this book.

"C'est un homme!"